NOW WHAT DO I DO ?

NOW WHAT DO I DO ?

A Guide to Help Teenagers with Their Parents' Separation or Divorce

Lynn Cassella-Kapusinski

acta

PUBLICATIONS

NOW WHAT DO I DO?
A Guide to Help Teenagers with Their Parents' Separation or Divorce
by Lynn Cassella-Kapusinski

Edited by Marcia Broucek
Cover design by Tom A. Wright
Text design and typesetting by Patricia Lynch

All Scripture quotations are from the *New Revised Standard Version Bible*,
copyright © 1989 by the Division of Christian Education of the National Council
of the Churches of Christ in the USA. Used by permission.

Published by ACTA Publications, 5559 W. Howard Street, Skokie, IL 60077
(800) 397-2282 www.actapublications.com.

Library of Congress Number: 2006925715
ISBN 10: 0-87946-304-X
ISBN 13: 978-0-87946-304-5
Printed in the United States of America
Year: 15 14 13 12 10 9 8 7 6
Printing: 10 9 8 7 6 5 4 3 2

CONTENTS

CHAPTER ONE

Feeling Bummed Out: How Do You Deal with It?

CHAPTER TWO

Blame: Whose Fault Is It Anyway?

CHAPTER THREE

Self-Esteem: Am I Any Good?

*I know how important it is to have a guide
when your parents separate and divorce.
With love, I dedicate this book to that special person in my life.*

*To my older brother, Marc, for the countless hours
you spent talking with me and watching over me.
Your "little sister" continues to admire you
and listen to all of your advice.
You have done more good for me than you will ever know.*

A Note to the Reader

If you are like me, maybe you wondered for a long time if your parents might separate or divorce someday. Maybe they fought too much or stopped spending time together. Or perhaps one of them was unfaithful or had a serious problem and didn't get help for it. Their troubles may have created so much tension that you even felt relieved when they broke up.

What you likely didn't predict though—whether your parents separated recently or divorced years ago—are all the difficulties that would result. This book is here to help you through them. I wrote it because I learned some things from my own parents' divorce. And I want to share them with you so your journey may be easier.

I hope this book will help you tell your story and learn from it. Why is that important? Because if you don't, those thoughts and feelings that you stuff down will explode later like a volcano. All that hot rock and steam—feelings like anger, sadness and shame—will eventually spill out in ways that hurt others and yourself. It's like when you get sick and need to go to the doctor, take medicine and get plenty of rest. If you don't take care of yourself, your sickness gets worse. It's the same way with hurtful situations. You need to take care of yourself by getting the hurt out. Otherwise, your problems get worse.

This book also has fun exercises and activities that you can do alone or with friends. You will learn a lot about yourself and soon realize something really important: It *is* possible to get through this difficulty and make it work for you.

In this book I also share what happened to me when my parents separated and divorced. Your situation probably differs from mine. However, I hope you will feel that someone understands what you're going through. I hope it helps you feel less alone. I also hope that some of the things that helped me will help you find peace. Life *can* get better when you "take charge" of your problems.

God has a big part in this book also. Maybe you don't trust that God is there for you. You may even find it difficult to believe in God right now. Whatever your feelings or religious background may be, I strongly encourage you to give God a chance. My life didn't move on until I allowed God to help me.

So, may God bless you and…here we go!

—Lynn Cassella-Kapusinski

Feeling Bummed Out: How Do You Deal with It?

"Hey, what's up? Is your dad coming to graduation?"

"He can't," I say. "He'll be in Europe for a conference. It's not a big deal, though." I look away. There's no way I'm going to tell my friend that my parents have separated.

"Not a big deal? You're graduating with highest honors! I'd be so upset if my dad couldn't be there."

"Yeah, but my dad will probably bring me lots of gifts just to make up for it." I force a smile.

My friend nods, but says nothing.

He will be there some day, says a voice inside my head, even though a part of me doesn't believe it. I wish I could tell my friend the real truth: My dad moved out for good, and I don't know when I'll hear from him again.

Some days I wonder if he will ever be involved in my life again. But then I remember how he used to talk with me and how he let me work in his office, and I know there's no way he will stay away for good. Besides, I have to have hope.

"At least you don't have to worry about him embarrassing you," my friend says with a frown. "My dad always takes so many stupid pictures."

I nod as if I understand, but inside I wonder if my dad has a picture of me anywhere. "I've got to see what Mr. Moser wants," I say, quickly changing the subject. "It's about our next student council meeting," I throw in before heading to the principal's office. I check the empty student council mailbox and start talking with Mr. Moser's secretary, just in case anyone's watching.

Sorting It Out

My dad left home when I was eleven. I don't remember anything about that day or the days that followed. All I remember is that he moved to a nearby town for a short while, then out of state. He kept moving farther away, eventually settling in a town across country. I talked with him less and less and was never sure when I'd see him. It hurt a lot because I felt as if I didn't have a dad anymore.

I tried not to think about it, though. Instead, I told myself what I wanted to hear: that it was just a matter of time before my dad would come back into my life for good. However, as time passed, nothing improved with my dad, and I became angry about it. I didn't feel safe expressing my anger out in the open, so I channeled it into school work and became overly competitive. Yet this led only to more wishful thinking and denial. I kept telling myself, *Once I accomplish more, Dad will pay more attention to me.*

No matter how much I distracted myself, though, I still felt bummed out. One feeling that haunted me was rejection. I couldn't understand why my dad didn't contact me more often. *Was there something wrong with me?* I decided there must be. I felt like the biggest loser in the world.

Maybe you're feeling bummed out because you don't see one of your parents much anymore. Perhaps your parents have put you in the middle of their fighting. Or you might have a stepparent whom you can't get along with, or a parent who has a serious personal problem, such as an alcohol or drug addiction. Or maybe you feel as if you've gotten a rotten deal all the way around.

Everyone feels bummed out when parents separate or divorce. It's part of being human. The important place to start is to acknowledge that you have these feelings.

1. YOUR FEELINGS CHECKLIST

Check (✓) any feelings you have about your parents' separation/divorce/remarriage or about the way your parent(s) is treating you.

NEGATIVE FEELINGS:

- ☐ afraid
- ☐ angry
- ☐ angry at God
- ☐ ashamed
- ☐ confused
- ☐ disappointed
- ☐ discouraged
- ☐ disgusted
- ☐ distrustful
- ☐ embarrassed
- ☐ guilty
- ☐ jealous
- ☐ lonely
- ☐ rejected
- ☐ sad
- ☐ unforgiving
- ☐ worried

POSITIVE FEELINGS:

- ☐ better loved by a parent(s)
- ☐ closer to God
- ☐ compassionate
- ☐ more mature
- ☐ more understanding
- ☐ relieved
- ☐ sympathetic
- ☐ thoughtful

other negative feelings:

_____

_____

_____

_____

_____

_____

_____

_____

_____

other positive feelings:

_____

_____

_____

_____

_____

_____

_____

_____

_____

Choose one of the negative feelings you checked and fill in the following.

I feel _____ when I *[describe a situation]*

_____

_____

_____

_____

_____

When I feel _____ I *[describe what you do]*

_____

_____

_____

_____

_____

Dealing with It

Everyone copes with bummed-out feelings in different ways. My strategy was to try and get rid of them by achieving as much as I could. But no matter how much I accomplished, the feelings always came back. They followed me everywhere like a dark cloud that kept saying, "You're not good enough. You'll never be good enough."

2. GETTING A GRIP

Check (✓) any of the things that you usually do when you're feeling bummed out.

- ❐ watch a lot of TV or play video games
- ❐ mope around
- ❐ yell, pick a fight, or have a tantrum
- ❐ bully others
- ❐ cry
- ❐ pig out
- ❐ hurt myself
- ❐ engage in sexual activity
- ❐ use drugs or alcohol, or smoke cigarettes
- ❐ try to fight them off by achieving (for example, by trying to get good grades or do really well in sports)
- ❐ gamble
- ❐ drive recklessly
- ❐ talk with someone about how I'm feeling (either in person, on the phone or online)
- ❐ talk with God
- ❐ talk with a pet
- ❐ write about how I feel
- ❐ work out
- ❐ express my feelings creatively (for example, by drawing or playing an instrument)

Take a look at the things you checked. Those in the right column are constructive ways to deal with negative feelings. Those in the left column are not. Instead, they are things you might be doing to avoid your feelings. After all, when you feel bummed out, it makes life more difficult. You might even try to convince yourself that your situation *is no big deal* or that you *don't care* when, deep down, you don't really believe either statement. Or you may try to throw your bummed-out feelings at someone else, only to find that they come back like a boomerang.

You might be able to avoid feeling bummed out in the short run. However, you can't avoid these feelings in the long run. It's impossible to make your feelings go away for good. You may be able to send them underground for a while, but they will always find a way to resurface. The truth is, the more you try to bury them, the more power they will have over you, taking more control and causing worse problems. For example, some teenagers end up doing worse and worse in school, then find they can't get into college or get a good job later on. Or they may get into trouble with teachers or the law, or get involved with drugs or sex and end up missing out on opportunities to build a good life for themselves.

3. YOUR "GRIP GRADE"

Look back at the things you checked in "2. Getting a Grip." Now, imagine that your best friend is doing these things. What grade would you give to describe how well your friend is coping? Write a few lines about ways these actions could help or hurt your friend.

GRIP GRADE: _____

_____

_____

_____

_____

_____

_____

What Are Your Options?

Whatever your "grip grade," there are things you can do to improve it. Finding healthy ways to deal with your feelings is like taking care of a car so it runs well, keeps you safe, and lasts a long time. In much the same way, you need to take care of your emotions so that they serve you well.

4. FEELINGS TUNE-UP

Here are some things to help you work through your bummed-out feelings. Check (✓) any that you already do. Put a plus (+) by any that seem worth a try.

❏ **Write about how you feel (for example, keep a journal, write a blog, or write a poem, story or song).**

Bad feelings often become less powerful when you write them out. You don't have to show anyone what you write, unless you want to. Give yourself permission to rip up or delete what you write. The important thing is to express your feelings.

❏ **Record your feelings.**

You might find it easier to talk out your feelings than to write them down. If so, it can help to record what you say, then play it back. Not only will it help you feel better, but you might hear something in what you say that needs attention, such as an irrational belief. You can then erase the recording if you want to.

❏ **Draw or paint a picture of how you feel.**

Sometimes it is difficult to express feelings in words. You might find it helpful to get a large pad on which to draw. Don't worry about how it looks. Use shapes and colors and texture to convey what's going on for you.

❏ **Work out or play sports.**

Much has been written about the benefits of endorphins that get released through exercise. Endorphins make us feel better, improve our mood, increase pleasure and minimize pain. Exercise can lift your spirits and help you feel better about yourself.

❏ **Talk with someone you trust or join a support/discussion group.**

Talking about what you're going through with a close friend or an adult whom you trust is a good way to handle feeling bummed out. Another person can ask helpful questions or share similar experiences that may help you understand your feelings and feel less alone.

❏ **Ask your parents questions.**

If there's something you don't understand—such as why your parents really had to separate or divorce—ask your parents to tell you more about it. It won't take away the hurt, but it may help you understand more of the truth. It might also prevent you from taking sides, blaming yourself, or wishing for things that probably won't come true.

❏ **Realize and accept what you can't change about your parent(s). Find a positive role model (such as a coach, teacher, aunt or uncle) to interact with.**

We all deserve to have parents who take seriously the job of raising, loving and protecting us. Unfortunately, though, not all parents accept this responsibility. If you have a parent who acts like a "bad parent" time and time again (for example, not keeping promises, not seeing or calling you, not providing for you, etc.), you need to accept what you cannot change about him or her. Look for a positive role model, some-one on whom you can depend, who will be your friend. You deserve some support in this tough time.

❏ **Let yourself cry.**

There are all kinds of losses to accept when parents breakup. Crying is not a sign of weakness; it is a release of grief. Crying relieves stress, reduces hormone and chemical levels in the body, and can help you return to a calmer state.

One More Important Option

Maybe you feel as if nothing will help. Maybe you've tried some things but nothing seems to make you feel any better. There is one more important option: Think about your relationship with God.

Maybe you're mad at God, or you've been ignoring God, or you believe that God is not really there for you. I believe God gently and insistently invites us to share these feelings, no matter what they are. Once we do, God has a better chance to strengthen and direct us. Imagine putting the "rocks" of your feelings into God's hands. You might be surprised at the "diamonds" God gives back to you.

5. GIVING IT TO GOD

Give your bummed-out feelings to God by writing a note or drawing a picture below.

Understanding Grief

Do you ever wonder if you're "normal" because you have so many different feelings about your parents' breakup or the changes in your relationship with them? Do you ever feel as if you might feel bummed out forever? If so, understanding the grief process can help.

You have probably heard about the stages of grief that people experience when a loved one dies. In her landmark book, *On Death and Dying*, Elizabeth Kubler-Ross identified five stages of grief:

- Denial (and isolation): "This isn't *happening* to me!"
- Anger: "Why is this happening to *me*?"
- Bargaining (or deal making): "I promise I'll be a better person if…"
- Depression: "I don't *care* anymore."
- Acceptance: "I'm *ready* for whatever comes."

All kinds of losses happen when parents separate or divorce, and these stages of grief apply to these losses just as they do to death.

What have you lost? Maybe you have less contact now with your parent who has moved out. Or you may have more responsibilities for your younger siblings, or there may be less money available for you. Your family may have had to move to a new neighborhood and, in addition to having a smaller room, you might see your friends less often.

You will probably experience each stage of grief at some time during and after your parents' divorce. But, like me, you might not move through the stages in any exact order. Instead, you might "bump around," even go in reverse. In other words, you might feel emotions that you thought you had gotten over.

This happened to me. For a long time, I bargained. I thought, *If I get good grades in school, Dad will show more interest in me.* I was able to get the grades, but it didn't change my dad's behavior. Then, I jumped back to my angry feelings: *This is so wrong and unfair.* Sometimes, I went in reverse and denied my feelings: *I'm probably just overreacting. Maybe this really isn't as bad as I think.* It's normal to go in reverse and experience feelings from before. You might also feel stuck in a stage, as if you're riding in a car that keeps stalling.

In my case, I didn't want to face the fact that my dad could not love me in the ways I needed most. So, I chose to stay stuck in denial. I was afraid to see who my dad was because that meant facing a huge loss. So I blamed myself and saw only what I wanted to see.

Maybe you, too, are blaming yourself or wishing blindly for something from your parents. Or maybe you're so angry at one (or both) of them that you doubt your feelings will ever change. If so, know that it's normal to be stuck in a feeling. It simply means that you're not ready yet to take the next step.

There's no required timetable for moving through grief. It's not like having to pass algebra so you can move onto geometry. You will move through grief at your own pace and in your own way.

6. YOUR GRIEF JOURNEY

On the circle below, draw a stick figure or symbol that shows where you are right now in your grief journey. Then write a note on the next page about your current feelings.

DENIAL & ISOLATION
This really isn't happening.
This isn't a big deal.
If anyone asks me about it,
I'll just change the subject.

ACCEPTANCE
I wish things could be different,
but I've accepted it.
I'm going to get through this.
Some good things have resulted
from all this.

BARGAINING
Maybe if I do X, Dad/Mom will pay
attention to me.
If I get into trouble, maybe Dad and
Mom will get back together.
I'll make Dad/Mom feel so guilty that
he/she will have to move back home.

DEPRESSION
No one cares about me anymore.
I'll never feel better again.
I'm worthless.

ANGER
This is all my mom/dad's fault.
I hate my life.
I'll never trust anyone again.

MY CURRENT FEELINGS

A Reality Check

The hard truth is that you may never heal completely from your grief. However, your attitude about your grief can help you move through it.

Perhaps you have been taught that grief is a private matter. Or that God comforts the grieving. Or that tears are the *only* expression of grief. Knowing how you think about grief will help you learn how to live through grief.

7. GOT AN ATTITUDE?

What's your "grief attitude"? Circle "true" or "false" for each statement below.

a) **People only feel grief when someone dies.**	True	False
b) **If you replace a loss, your grief will go away.**	True	False
(For example, if I get a new dog, it will make me feel better about my dog that just died.)		
c) **You have to feel grief in order to heal.**	True	False
d) **Grief eventually ends.**	True	False
e) **Keeping super busy can help you get through grief.**	True	False
f) **You should express grief only in private.**	True	False
g) **When someone is expressing grief, you should leave him/her alone.**	True	False

Check it out. How does what you think add up?

a) **People only feel grief when someone dies.**

FALSE. We feel grief about *all* losses.

b) **If you replace a loss, your grief will go away.**

FALSE. Each relationship is unique. This makes it impossible to replace our losses.

c) **You have to feel grief in order to heal.**

TRUE. Grief will not go away if we ignore it. Instead, it will snowball and affect us in worse ways. We need to keep expressing our feelings in order to be healed of them.

d) **Grief eventually ends.**

FALSE. We never fully separate from our losses. Instead, over time, we can learn to live with loss.

e) **Keeping super busy can help you get through grief.**

FALSE. It can prevent you from feeling grief and, thus, getting through it.

f) **You should express grief only in private.**

FALSE. We cannot control when and where we feel grief.

g) **When someone is expressing grief, you should leave him/her alone.**

FALSE. We need to share our grief with others and receive support. This helps us move through grief.

It takes most teenagers a long time—years, if not decades—before grieving turns into healing. It's like having your leg badly injured in a sporting event, then having to have surgery and years of physical therapy. You might always feel some pain whenever it gets humid and rainy. However, your leg will get stronger as you exercise and take care of it. It's the same with the pain of your parents' divorce. Be patient with yourself. Seek as much encouragement and support as you can. You might be surprised at the strength you discover in yourself that you never knew you had. Chances are you'll become an even better person than you were before.

You have two choices. One leads to giving up. The other leads to growing. When you keep thinking, *"Poor me. Life is so unfair. I am powerless,"* you are giving up. When you choose a healthy attitude about grief, you will be able to grow from grief. You will find reasons to be hopeful. You will recognize that, although life is tough right now, you have power. You will realize that your hurts don't have to last forever. You can look to the present and future as opportunities to grow. And you can accept help from others. This is the choice that will create wholeness.

8. EXTRA WAYS TO HELP YOURSELF

- In a journal or sketch book, write or draw something about your strongest desire(s) regarding your parent(s) or family situation. Consider what you wrote or drew. Is there a wish or a hope in it? It's important to make the distinction. A wish is a fantasy, whereas a hope has some reality to it. Write your response in your journal. If you're unsure, write about that.

- Make time to talk with God on a daily basis about whatever you need to. Try it for at least one week; then consider the effect it has had on you.

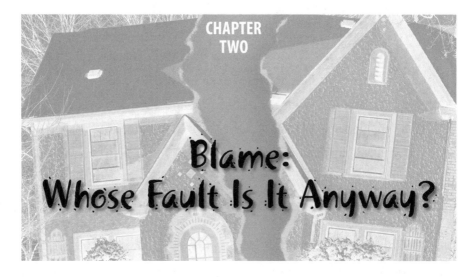

CHAPTER TWO

Blame: Whose Fault Is It Anyway?

Lisa hears something tap the window. She gets up from the piano and looks outside, but everything looks the same. She stands there with her arms folded, watching the cars zoom past on the busy parkway in front of her house. Everyone seems to know where they're going, but not her.

She still doesn't know why her parents had to get a divorce. *Couldn't they have worked out their problems if they had gone to counseling? Did they really try hard enough?*

She sits back down at the piano and turns to Chopin's *Prelude in D-flat Major.* She positions her fingers above the keys and plays the tranquil melody. She remembers the last conversation she heard between her parents. They were fighting about her grades. Her dad said they weren't good enough. Then he went on to blame her mother because she let Lisa spend so much time talking on the telephone and hanging out at the mall. He also said Lisa should be doing more chores, especially cleaning her messy room.

Maybe if she had worked harder and been the type of daughter her dad had wanted, none of her parents' problems would have started.

The melody changes. It can't be *all* her fault. Her parents had been fighting for years. They must have fought about other things besides her.

She moves her right thumb up to hit the black G-sharp key over and over. Maybe she should have told her dad she loved him more often. Maybe that would have given him a reason to stay.

She plays the original melody again. She should have done more to try and fix things.

The melody softens. She wishes she knew more about why they had to get a divorce, so she wouldn't feel so confused all the time.

She stops playing, even though she hasn't finished the piece. She pulls the cover over the keyboard and turns off the piano light.

The Blame Game

When my parents separated, I didn't concern myself with finding out the facts. It didn't matter to me what each parent did or who was more "right" or more "wrong." All I cared about was seeing my dad again. That didn't happen, though, for a long time, and my relationship with him grew only more uncertain. When it became too much for me to handle, all I knew was that the situation was someone's fault.

Blaming is often an automatic reaction. It's easy to blame a parent or someone or something else when you're upset about the changes that the separation or divorce brings. Blaming can also serve as a quick fix that leaves you feeling more in control. This is especially tempting if you feel you have no say in the decisions that your parents are making.

1. HOW DO YOU SEE IT?

When there's a problem, what's your first reaction? Circle one letter for each question.

1) **If Lisa were your friend, which of these statements would you most likely say to her?**

   a. "I'm glad I'm not the only one. I often feel guilty about the way things are."

   b. "Stop beating yourself up. This is a problem between your parents. They are responsible for it, not you."

   c. "The divorce is probably your dad's fault. He should get a clue and not be so strict."

   d. "God owes you an explanation. I'd ask him why he took your dad away."

2) **Your gut reaction to your parents' separation or divorce is:**

   a. Maybe there's something I could have done (or could do) to change things.

   b. Mom and Dad are the ones who have to work out their problems. I'm staying out of it.

   c. I'm still pretty angry, especially at my mom/dad. If she/he had been more responsible, I wouldn't be in this mess.

   d. If God really loved me, he'd make my parents get back together (or make my parent a better parent).

3) Which of these statements best describes you:

   a. Succeeding in life is a lot like succeeding in school. You can get most anything you want, if you try hard enough.

   b. It's pretty easy for me to let go of a problem or situation I can't do anything about. You can control some things in life, but there's a lot you can't control, too.

   c. There is always someone at fault in every problem. Those who are at fault are often bad people.

   d. If I always try to be a good person, God will reward me with what I want.

4) Suppose two of your closest friends just had a really bad fight. How would you most likely respond to them?

   a. I would listen to what each has to say, then do my best to help them resolve their differences.

   b. I would be supportive of both of them. I wouldn't take sides, though, because I wouldn't want to lose either friend.

   c. I'd take the side of the friend whom I was closer to. That kind of loyalty is an important part of friendship.

   d. I'd take the side of the person who had a better moral character.

THE SELF-FROWNER: If you circled mostly a's, you're pretty hard on yourself. It's as if you're always frowning at yourself, telling yourself that you should be doing more. Blaming yourself when things go wrong is a seductive option because it lets you believe that you have power to fix things. The harder reality to face is that your parents' have shortcomings and make mistakes, that their separation or divorce is not of your making and is certainly beyond your fixing.

While you have good intentions, you need to accept what you can't control: other people's problems. It's time to start being good to yourself. Don't give into the false belief that you've caused any of this, because you haven't. Stay out of your parents' conflict and let them handle it.

STEADY EDDY: If you circled mostly b's, you are doing a good job of being fair, objective and faithful to your principles. While it might not be easy, you avoid taking one of your parent's sides, and you realize that only they can solve their problems. And you recognize what you can and cannot control. You don't jump to conclusions either. Instead, you try to get as many facts as possible before forming an opinion. Congratulations!

THE FIGHTER: If you circled mostly c's, your anger is controlling you. Maybe one parent has told you details about the separation or divorce that have turned you against the other. Or perhaps you've taken the side of the parent you feel you need to protect, or the one who treats you better. But a separation or divorce is not one person's fault. Rarely is there one "good guy" and one "bad guy." While one parent might seem to be more at fault than the other, both have some responsibility for the situation. Dumping all the blame on one parent isn't fair. It won't help you discover the truth, and it won't help you feel any better.

Taking anger out on your parent—or anyone else—is a destructive way of handling your feelings. While you may have good reason to be angry, the challenge is to find a constructive way to deal with those feelings. It starts with understanding your feelings and trying to forgive the parent with whom you're angry. This will help keep your anger from spilling over into all of your relationships and possibly jeopardizing friendships that could be supportive for you. (We'll look at this more in Chapter 8 on anger.)

THE GOD-DUMPER : If you circled mostly d's, you're quick to blame God when things go wrong. You probably have a strong sense of right and wrong, which is good. You may get angry at God a lot, too, which is okay because God understands. The problem you run into is the common belief that God causes bad things to happen. When we're in the middle of something bad, we tend to ask, "Why me? Why did God let this happen?"

Here's something very important to consider: God doesn't make bad things happen. Rather, God is a loving God and, out of love, gives us free will. And because of this, everyone is free to make choices and so to make mistakes.

God doesn't promise anyone a problem-free life, no matter how good we are. What God offers, instead, is strength and direction to cope with our problems and grow from them. (We'll talk more about this in Chapter 9 on God.)

"It's *My* Fault!"

When my parents divorced, I never really thought they would get back to-gether. I did, however, believe that my father would one day become more involved in my life again. That never happened, though, and I couldn't understand it.

For a long time, I blamed myself. I thought my dad's behavior was my fault. I thought I had to earn his attention by being a perfect daughter: never get into trouble, never get angry at him, do everything I was supposed to do. I managed to do all these things, but it didn't change anything.

As time went on, my hurt grew even bigger than my confusion. I started to take my parents' separation personally, as if it meant they didn't love *me* anymore. Maybe you, too, have thought this: *If my parents really loved me, they would have tried harder to make their marriage work.* Perhaps you think less of yourself now, as if you're doomed to fail because of their divorce.

Here's the most important thing you can understand about your parents' breakup: The problems between your parents are *never* about you. Separation or divorce doesn't mean your parents love you any less. It concerns only their feelings toward each other, not toward you.

Just as you were not responsible for your parents' marriage, neither are you responsible for their separation or divorce. Maybe you've heard your parents arguing about you, or maybe they're having a court battle about custody or child-support payments. When the main topic of your parents' arguments is you, it's easy to think the problems are all your fault. However, they never are.

Consider friends who have disappointed you. Have you ever had a friend dump you because he or she wanted to be friends with someone more popular? Maybe this person had even been your best friend. You really wanted to stay friends with him or her and did all you could to be a good friend, but still things didn't work out. You're left feeling hurt and angry, right?

Unfortunately, despite our trying to do our best, people let us down. It's often easier to blame ourselves when this happens than to see the other person's shortcomings. However, we need to remember that the situation isn't about who we are or what we've done (or not done). Rather, it's about who that person is.

Where do you stand with all this? When you're really honest with yourself, what thoughts do you have about being responsible for your parents' breakup?

2. WHERE DO YOU FIT IN?

Do you think you have done anything that might have contributed to your parents' breakup? If "yes," explain.

_____

_____

_____

_____

_____

_____

_____

Is there anything that you think you could or should do to help solve the problems between your parents? If "yes," explain.

_____

_____

_____

_____

_____

_____

_____

"It's *Their* Fault!"

Even if you're not blaming yourself, you're probably feeling powerless about the separation or divorce. One of the common ways people fight feeling helpless is to try to gain control by taking sides.

When my dad left, I wanted to throw my hurt and anger at him, but he wasn't there. Even when I did talk with him, I was afraid to show my real feelings because I feared it might cause him to desert me for good.

My feelings had to go somewhere, though. Since I couldn't dump them on my dad, I threw them at my mom. It was easy to blame her because I felt "safe" with her. I knew she would never leave me. So I blamed her for everything my dad wasn't doing, as well as for the whole divorce thing.

What about you? Do you place all (or most of) the blame for your parents' breakup on either your mom or dad? If you're not sure, consider these questions: Did one parent make work or another relationship a higher priority than the marriage? Did she or he often say or do mean things that hurt your other parent? Did your parent refuse to get help for a personal problem?

Give yourself a few minutes to respond to the following question.

3. WHOM DO YOU BLAME?

Ask yourself, "Which parent do I blame the most?" List some of your reasons for blaming this parent.

I blame my _____ **the most because:**

1. _____

2. _____

3. _____

4. _____

5. _____

6. _____

One of the reasons I blamed my mom was because I was too afraid to see my dad's weaknesses. If I saw them, then I would have to see the ways he couldn't be there for me. And I was too afraid to handle that pain.

Most of us don't want to see our parents' shortcomings. Or we tend to overlook them because a parent gives us special treatment, such as money and gifts or no curfew. But the truth is, all humans are flawed. As I got to know my dad better, I saw more and more how his weaknesses hindered him from making good choices. These same flaws contributed to the failures in my parents' marriage. This didn't change the fact that my dad was a good person who was trying as best as he knew how. He wasn't a bad or evil person. Instead, he was a person who had weaknesses, like we all do.

Seeing my dad's weaknesses made my loss of him more real. It also challenged me to grow. It hurt a lot and was very scary. However, facing this truth helped me find peace and move on with my life. It also helped me better understand why my parents got divorced.

Consider the parent you blame less or not at all.

4. IT TAKES TWO

Ask yourself, "Which parent do I blame the least?" Consider what mistakes this parent may have made in the marriage and list some of his or her weaknesses.

I blame my _____ the least because:

1. _____

2. _____

3. _____

4. _____

5. _____

6. _____

"Why Did This Have to Happen?"

When your parents married, they didn't plan on getting separated or divorced. What often happens, though, is that people marry without being ready or prepared to make such an important commitment. It would be like skipping high school and going straight into college. While it might be possible, it's likely that someone making this leap will flunk out.

Sometimes people marry for the wrong reasons. And sometimes people just can't live up to expectations—theirs or their partners'. Most of the time, separation and divorce happens for several different reasons. Any one of them can cause the love between a husband and wife to wear away. Just as a plant that hasn't had enough water and sunlight dies, so too can your parents' marriage fail when they stop giving one another respect, attention and love.

Think about some of the friendships you've had. Maybe you joined the basketball team, band or cheerleading squad and became friends with new kids with whom you had more in common than your old friends. Or maybe an old friend joined a clique that you didn't like or one that didn't accept you. Whatever the reason, maybe new interests or values broke up the friendship. This same thing can happen between parents too.

5. WHAT'S THE "REAL DEAL?"

Take a look at this list of possible reasons why persons separate or divorce. Check (✓) any that apply to your parents. If you're not sure, check your best guess(es).

❒ **HAVING BLINDERS ON:** Maybe your parents married when they first fell in love. Their feelings may have been so strong that they ignored other factors that help make a marriage work, such as friendship, shared values and morals, good communication, and sensitivity to each other's feelings. They may have placed too much importance on being in love and mistakenly thought it would be enough.

Sometimes people ignore potential problems when they're dating because they want things to work out. Things like a violent temper, a bad drinking habit, or selfishness. When someone "has blinders on," she often thinks, *If I love him enough, he will change into the loving man I want him to be.* Unfortunately, this is unrealistic, wishful thinking that ignores the fact that people have to desire growth and change for themselves.

Does this apply to your parent(s)? ❒ yes   ❒ no
If "yes," which one? ❒ Mom   ❒ Dad   ❒ both

❐ **MARRYING TOO YOUNG:** Statistics show that the divorce rate is highest for those who marry at age twenty-five or younger. Why is age important? Because when a person is older, he or she usually is more ready to make a serious commitment. And when people marry too young, they can develop completely different interests as they mature and find that they have very little in common. Older persons often know themselves and what they want from life a lot better. They're often more mature and willing to make the sacrifices required in marriage.

Does this apply to your parent(s)? ❐ yes ❐ no
If "yes," which one? ❐ Mom ❐ Dad ❐ both

❐ **CARRYING OLD BAGGAGE:** If one (or both) of your parents got married without having worked through a difficult hurt or loss in the past—such as a previous divorce, the death of a loved one, a major illness or injury—then your parent brought "baggage" to the marriage. It would be like carrying an overstuffed suitcase all the time, one you had to sit on in order to shut. Old "baggage" might cause angry outbursts or poor decision-making. It might keep your parents distant from each other.

Sometimes people are unable to resolve a big hurt that occurs during their marriage as well. If there's a death in the family, or a loss of a job, or some other major crisis, a marriage that's already in trouble may not be able to survive the stress.

Does this apply to your parent(s)? ❐ yes ❐ no
If "yes," which one? ❐ Mom ❐ Dad ❐ both

❐ **HAVING AN AFFAIR:** Maybe one of your parents is not being faithful to the other. Sex can be a very powerful, destructive force in a relationship. This may not be an area your parents share with you, but you may sense that this is a problem between them.

Does this apply to your parent(s)?   ❐ yes   ❐ no
If "yes," which one?   ❐ Mom   ❐ Dad   ❐ both

❐ **DIFFERING NEEDS:** Maybe one of your parents is extremely jealous or possessive, which makes the other parent feel controlled and smothered. Or one parent may have a hobby that consumes a great deal of time, leaving the other parent feeling neglected. Maybe one parent likes a lot of socialization and the other needs more alone time. Or perhaps one parent wants to move to a new location and the other wants to stay put. All of these point to a basic difference in what each person needs or wants and can cause serious rifts in a relationship.

Does this apply to your parent(s)?   ❐ yes   ❐ no
If "yes," which one?   ❐ Mom   ❐ Dad   ❐ both

❐ **MORE REASONS:** There are many other reasons why people separate and divorce. Check (✓) any of the following that apply to your parents. If you're not sure, write "NS."

____   problems with alcohol or drugs
____   depression or other mental health problem
____   frequent gambling
____   criminal activity
____   physical, emotional and/or sexual abuse
____   homosexuality
____   inability to get or hold a job

_____ inability to resolve conflicts regarding religion, money and/or childrearing

_____ other:

_____

_____

Are There Secrets?

When my parents separated, they never sat me and my brothers down to tell us they were getting a divorce. It was just something we *knew* was going to happen sooner or later. They fought too often, and their fights were only getting worse.

When they finally separated, it was a big relief because we no longer had to live with so much tension day in and day out. Yet the silence also haunted us. I had so many questions and too few answers. One of my most pressing questions was, *Why couldn't Mom and Dad have worked things out?* After all, they had been married for a long time. I didn't understand how love could die, especially after years.

Maybe you're not sure what caused your parents' separation or divorce because neither of your parents has talked with you about it. It's okay to ask. You might also try talking with an older sibling, relative or close friend of both your parents about the situation too.

Brace yourself, though, because you may get different reasons from each person you ask. Your question might lead to some bad-mouthing as well. However, it's still worth trying, because you might get information that will allow you to find out more of the truth.

6. PLAYING DETECTIVE

Do you have questions about your parents' breakup? If "yes," note them below.

---

7. EXTRA WAYS YOU CAN HELP YOURSELF

- Has your parents' separation or divorce changed the way you feel about yourself? If "yes," write a letter to your best friend about this. (Don't worry…you won't have to send it!) Next, imagine being your best friend and write a response to yourself.

- Have you been avoiding one of your parents because you blame him or her for the breakup? If so, spend time getting to know this parent better and try to put yourself in his or her shoes. Ask God to help you open your heart so you can see this parent's goodness instead of his or her failings. Notice any changes in your relationship as a result.

- Review the list of possible reasons in **"5. What's the Real Deal?"** with each of your parents. Ask them to help you understand more about what caused their breakup.

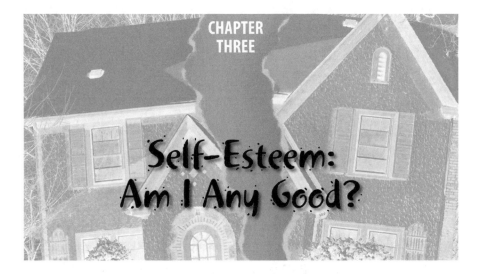

CHAPTER THREE

Self-Esteem: Am I Any Good?

I step off the plane and onto the walkway, holding my carry-on bag. My heart pounds hard against my chest. My mouth feels totally parched. *Dad is in the airport, waiting at the security area, and I'm going to see him in just a few minutes.* I walk through the gate, then down the long hallway toward baggage claim. My body feels tense all over.

I walk on, soon seeing the metal detectors and x-ray scanners a short distance ahead. I slow down on purpose and wait for a group of people to pass. Then I hurry behind them, staying close so I don't stand out.

Dad is standing straight ahead, dressed in a blue suit and tie. He looks the same as I remember: thick, black hair combed back neatly on all sides, clean-shaven, small hazel-colored eyes. His face hasn't changed, only aged.

He raises his hand and signals me over. I can't help but smile. I feel so happy, like everything might go my way this time. I swallow the lump in my throat as I approach.

"Good flight?" he asks.

"Yeah, very smooth. I had a window seat." I want to thank him for buy-

53

ing me the ticket, but I'm too afraid. I don't know how he'd respond. So, instead, I lamely add, "It's great to fly."

He reaches for my carry-on. "Here, let me take that."

"Are you sure?" I fold my arms and start biting my fingernails. It's strange having Dad pay attention to me. Maybe he really *is* happy to have me here. Maybe he's been missing me as much as I've missed him.

"Are you hungry?" he asks.

I haven't eaten anything all day except a snack on the plane, and I'm starving. But I casually turn it back on him: "What about you? Have you eaten?"

"I'm fine. I got here a little early, so I just grabbed a sandwich."

"Yeah, I'm good too."

We head to baggage claim, then the parking lot. During the ride to his house, Dad talks about his clients and coworkers and what's been happening in the local news. I look out the window at all the flat, barren land around. Lots of empty, open spaces. I feel like a hitchhiker he's just picked up.

"So, do you like animals?" Dad asks after a while.

"Yeah…" I respond slowly, wondering where this is going.

"Good, because I have a lot of them in the house. I've gotten pretty fond of them, actually. They all like their special dose of attention. Freddie, the Persian cat, likes to sit right on my desk when I'm paying the bills. And Sam, the poodle, likes to have his belly rubbed when I'm watching TV."

Dad, playing with animals? I remember all the times he sat in our family room alone, with the door locked, listening to music, never letting our dog in.

"They get the finest medicines too," he goes on, telling me about their latest trip to the vet. He knows more about the health of these animals than he does about mine! Is he completely clueless? I try to take an interest in what he's saying, but I keep thinking this is all so weird.

Dad stops to pay a toll. As he searches for change, I notice a homeless young man sitting at the side of the road. He's wearing a sign that says in large black letters: "Homeless. Trying to get something to eat. God bless you." I wonder if Dad would come looking for me if I were homeless.

"Hey…you okay over there?"

"Yeah…" I don't want him to think I'm being rude by not talking, so I add, "How's your health been?"

He proceeds to tell me about the physical he just had and the results of his blood work. He explains his exercise routine, how much he weighs, and the diet he's trying to follow. I look back out the window.

He must think I'm pretty worthless, not to ask one question about my life. I guess I really don't matter all that much to him.

"They Don't Get It"

Each time I saw my dad, I thought, *This will be the visit where things will be different*. If he gave me the slightest bit of attention, I took it as a sign that he might become involved in my life. I clung desperately to the wish that he'd someday become the father I needed.

Time and time again, though, my hopes got squashed. Whenever I saw or heard from my dad, he talked only about his life and interests. He asked few, if any, questions about me. I felt angry and confused. He should have been taking more of an interest in me than himself! After all, he was the parent and I was the child.

1. WHAT'S YOUR WISH?

Write a few sentences about what you need most from your parents. For each parent, specify what he or she is doing or not doing to meet this need.

EXAMPLES:

"I need my dad to consider my feelings. He's always angry. It makes me clam up and feel as though I can't talk to him."

"I wish my mom would realize what my world's like right now. All she does is give me orders all the time. I need more freedom."

FROM MY DAD:

_____

_____

_____

_____

_____

FROM MY MOM:

_____

_____

_____

_____

_____

"It Must Be Me!"

I took my father's treatment of me very personally. I figured he thought I wasn't worth his time or energy. No matter what I did, I felt I'd never be good enough. Then I began to think no decent guy would ever date me, that I'd never be able to do anything worthwhile in life.

Maybe your situation is different, and both your parents are treating you as parents should. Even in this situation, though, you might still feel doomed to failure simply because your parents separated or divorced. You might, for example, think that since your parents' marriage didn't work you'll never be able to make marriage work for you. You might feel embarrassed by the breakup or by your parents' lifestyle after it. It's easy to take personally what your parents do or don't do.

2. TAKING IT PERSONALLY

Has your parents' breakup stirred up any negative thoughts and feelings about yourself? If so, write or draw a picture about this.

"What I Really Think"

I never told anyone how worthless I felt. Instead, I tried to rid these feelings by becoming an overachiever. Each time I accomplished something, I could tell myself, *Yeah, you're okay.* However, that belief was temporary. It lasted only until the next test or competition; then I'd have to prove myself all over again. I was caught in a vicious cycle that never helped me feel better about myself. My self-esteem was trashed.

3. WHAT'S HAPPENING?

How's your self-esteem these days? Check it out. After each statement in the first column, write "A" if you Agree or "D" if you Disagree.

	"A" or "D"	POINTS
1. I get along with most people.	_____	_____
2. I'm doing my best at school.	_____	_____
3. When people criticize me, I get angry.	_____	_____
4. I sometimes drink alcohol or do drugs when my friends pressure me.	_____	_____
5. When I fight with my friends or siblings and get into trouble for it, I say it was their fault, even when it wasn't.	_____	_____
6. I compliment others.	_____	_____
7. I follow rules easily.	_____	_____
8. I often say, "I don't know" or "I don't care."	_____	_____
9. I hate how I look.	_____	_____
10. My thoughts have value.	_____	_____
TOTAL		_____

Now give yourself the following points for each statement and write them in the "Points" column:

1. Agree.................2 points Disagree ....1 point	6. Agree ....2 points Disagree ....1 point
2. Agree ....2 points Disagree ....1 point	7. Agree.................2 points Disagree ....1 point
3. Agree.................1 point Disagree ....2 points	8. Agree.................1 point Disagree ....2 points
4. Agree ....1 point Disagree ....2 points	9. Agree.................1 point Disagree ....2 points
5. Agree ....1 point Disagree ....2 points	10. Agree ....2 points Disagree ....1 point

Then total your points:

20 points:	You have very strong self-esteem. Good for you!
17-19 points:	You're on the right path. Keep up the good work!
14-16 points:	There's a lot that's good about you, but you're not recognizing it.
10-13 points:	You're feeling low and overwhelmed. You need to take action to help yourself.

"Who I Really Am"

No one has perfect self-esteem. Even the most confident and successful people have doubts about themselves from time to time. This is natural and part of being human. None of us is perfect. However, when our parents fail to be good parents—whether it's before, during or after their divorce—our journey toward healthy self-esteem becomes even more difficult.

When my dad seemed not to notice me, I needed to separate who I was from how he treated me. I also needed to figure out ways to base my self-esteem not on externals but on who I was on the inside.

What about you? Are you falling into the trap of depending on people or things around you in order to feel good about yourself? Maybe some of these things are pretty important to you right now:

- looking good
- wearing expensive clothes
- having a boy/girlfriend
- being a "star" athlete
- being popular
- having money
- enjoying whatever status your parents have

While these things might make you feel decent about yourself for a while, basing self-esteem completely on externals never lasts in the long run. There will always be someone better looking, more popular, smarter, and so on than you are. When you start to play "the comparison game," you've already lost.

No matter how you feel about yourself, there is good in you. If you are having trouble seeing it, this is the time to find someone who can help you look at things a little differently. Talk with a trusted friend, or seek out an adult or counselor who can listen. Ask them for some accurate feedback about you. They can help you see that your good qualities—such as your sensitivity and responsible nature—haven't died. They will be able to help you see yourself for who you really are.

4. SO THEY SAY . . .

Ask a close friend or family member what he or she thinks is good about you. Write down what they tell you.

_____

_____

_____

_____

_____

There's one more important piece to this self-esteem puzzle. No matter how your parents or anyone else treats you, you are valuable in God's eyes. Depending on where you are in your faith journey right now, this may be hard to accept. But no matter what happens, hang on to this: You are made in God's image. This means that you are truly good, that you have dignity, that you are more special than you can even imagine. You never have to earn God's love, only trust it. Letting God love you will help you love yourself again.

5. SO GOD SAYS . . .

Imagine having a conversation with God. Ask how God sees you, then listen for God's voice in your heart. Write down what you hear God say.

_____

_____

_____

_____

_____

The next time you get discouraged or down on yourself, take a look at what you have written for **"4. So They Say…"** and **"5. So God Says…"** Use these to remind yourself just how special you are. Remember, the world wouldn't be the same without you.

6. EXTRA WAYS TO HELP YOURSELF

- Just because your life might be difficult now, that doesn't mean it always will be. In your journal, write about how you want your life to be in the future. For example: What career do you want to pursue? Will you marry and have children? Where do you want to live?

- Set a goal for yourself. Make sure it is realistic, specific and measurable, and has a deadline. For example: "I am going to get a job (such as babysitting, mowing lawns, shoveling snow) and work at it for at least two months, so I can have money to go to the movies and eat out with my friends, buy new clothes, and/or buy sports equipment."

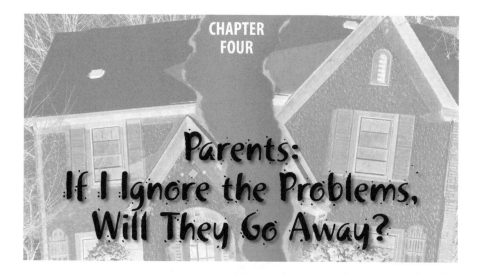

Parents:
If I Ignore the Problems,
Will They Go Away?

Rain smacks against my bedroom window. A huge clap of thunder shakes the house. A siren from an ambulance gets louder and louder, then fades away. Quiet fills my room again, but there's no way I can sleep.

I keep thinking about everything Dad said during our phone conversation: how he went on and on about his new girlfriend, and all the worry in his voice as he described her problems. I know I shouldn't be surprised at how much he cares for her. After all, it's been years since he left home. But his concern for her feels all wrong.

I continue hearing him, then slowly I feel myself fading, as if I don't exist. Maybe that's how Dad really thinks about me now that he has a girlfriend. Or maybe he just needs time to settle into his new life, and then he will be able to notice me.

I fade further. Then it hits me: I've never thought of my dad as caring for anyone else besides me. I guess I've never let myself see how needy he is either. It's as if I've never thought of him as being a separate person at all.

But, actually, my whole life he's been separate more than anything else.

The tears well up again. I can't believe I'm *still* crying about this! I feel as if he's leaving me all over again. And there's nothing I can do to stop it.

I give up and cry harder, as hard as I can, just to get all the ugly pain out.

When my sobs finally let up, I look across my room at the seashells on my bookcase. I get out of bed and rescue the broken ones from the bottom desk drawer. Slowly, I arrange them between the whole ones on the shelf.

I tell myself that nothing in life is perfect.

Connection Problems

My relationships with my parents changed in big ways after their separation. However, I kept denying the changes because they hurt a lot. My dad kept moving states and states away and didn't talk to me very often. Instead, he wrote letters. I was always so excited to find one in the mailbox. Yet each time I read one, I felt more left out because my dad talked only about himself and his new life apart from me. It was the same way when I saw him or talked with him on the phone. I felt like I couldn't connect with him.

How difficult is it for you to connect with your dad? Maybe he has more on his mind now and doesn't listen to you as much. Or maybe you don't get one-on-one time with him anymore because he has a girlfriend who is always there. Perhaps you haven't even seen your dad in months or years because he lives far away.

1. YOU AND YOUR DAD

On a scale from 1 to 10 (with 1 being much too close and 10 being far, far away), how close do you feel to your dad right now? Draw a circle around that number with "Dad" in it to show where he fits in the picture right now in relation to you.

$$\text{(ME)} \quad 1 \quad 2 \quad 3 \quad 4 \quad 5 \quad 6 \quad 7 \quad 8 \quad 9 \quad 10$$

As time went on, I kept wondering, *Did Dad stop loving me for good, or do I just need to be patient and wait for him to pull himself together?* I learned that neither the worst case nor the best case was true. The truth was somewhere in the middle: My dad did love me; he just couldn't love me in the ways I needed.

My relationship with my mom was the exact opposite. The separation squashed all space between us. However, I wanted so much for her to be happy that I took responsibility for her feelings. I thought I could take away her hurt by trying to please her all the time. However, this was just another way for me to deny the changes. It brought me worse problems, too, because it made me live more inside my mom's skin than my own.

Maybe your situation is similar. Or maybe it's the exact opposite. Maybe it's difficult to find a comfortable space with your mom. Perhaps she has to work longer hours now or is looking for a higher paying job and isn't home much. Or maybe she is having a tough time with the separation, so you're taking on more responsibility—perhaps too much—at home. Your mom might even be having such a tough time that she takes her anger out on you.

2. YOU AND YOUR MOM

On a scale from 1 to 10 (with 1 being much too close and 10 being far, far away), how close do you feel to your mom right now? Draw a circle around that number with "Mom" in it to show where she fits in the picture right now in relation to you.

(ME) 1   2   3   4   5   6   7   8   9   10

3. "DEAR PARENT"

Now, imagine talking to each of your parents about the space between you. On separate pieces of paper or on your computer, write one letter to your mom and one letter to your dad. Remember: These letters are for only you to see.

Start with the parent you feel furthest from. In the letter:

a) Tell your parent how you feel about the space between you.

b) Try to specify what your parent does—or doesn't do—that contributes to the space between you. You may draw a picture about this as well.

c) Include the thoughts/beliefs that you have—especially about yourself—as a result of your parent's actions or inactions.

Then write a second letter to the parent you feel closest to. In this letter:

a) Tell your parent how you feel about your relationship.

b) Try to specify what your parent does—or doesn't do—that encourages you to feel like you do.

c) Include the thoughts/beliefs that you have—especially about yourself—as a result of your parent's actions or inactions.

When you are finished with your letters, complete the lines below that fit for you:

My main problem with my dad is: _____

_____

The thoughts/beliefs I have about this problem are: _____

_____

I am trying to solve this problem by: _____

_____

It is/is not *[circle one]* **working because:** _____

_____

My main problem with my mom is: _____

_____

The thoughts/beliefs I have about this problem are: _____

_____

I am trying to solve this problem by: _____

_____

It is/is not *[circle one]* **working because:** _____

_____

Thought Problems

The thoughts and beliefs you have about your problems are really important because they influence how you go about solving them. For instance, if your thoughts and beliefs are irrational, you will likely become so stressed-out that you can't help but react in a destructive way. I did this a lot.

Because my dad didn't contact me often, I believed I was worthless. As a result of this irrational belief, I did nothing about my problem except conclude the worst about myself. It got me nowhere. Because my mom got upset and reprimanded me whenever I mentioned missing my dad, I believed I shouldn't feel sad and was being ungrateful if I had these feelings. This led to my unhealthy belief that negative feelings were bad and that I was bad for having them. This didn't serve me well either.

According to Dr. Albert Ellis, a clinical psychologist, irrational thoughts and beliefs have at least one of the following characteristics:

- Inflexible demands of yourself or others: You think in terms of "musts, absolutes, or shoulds."
- Awfulizing: You think, *It's awful, terrible, or horrible.*
- Low frustration tolerance: You tell yourself, *I can't stand it.*
- Poor rating of yourself or others: You conclude that you/he/she is bad or worthless.

Take another look at the thoughts/beliefs you noted above about your problems with your parents. Do those beliefs have any of these irrational characteristics? If so, you need to do a little work regarding them. Check out the questions on the next page developed by Dr. Ellis. They will help you take a more rational and realistic look at your beliefs.

4. GET REAL

Answer any of the following questions that apply to you.

Where is this thought/belief getting me? Is it helpful or self-defeating?
Where is the evidence to support the existence of this thought/belief?
Is my thought/belief logical?
Is this situation really as awful as I think it is?
Can I *really* not stand it?

_____

_____

_____

_____

_____

_____

Communication Problems

Irrational thoughts and beliefs can shut down communication faster than a bad cell phone connection. If, for example, you're thinking, *Why bother talking with my parents about this problem? They never listen anyway*, chances are this will become a self-fulfilling prophecy. You won't talk, they won't hear you, and the opportunity to work out a problem is history.

Or maybe you feel that talking with your parent will only harm your relationship. I was always too scared to confront my dad. I had so little contact with him that I was afraid I might say something that would cause him to reject me for good. It took me a long time to find the courage to approach him and, when I did, I did a lousy job. I either questioned him like a prosecuting attorney, or I got so angry that I did something destructive such as throwing things at him. Yet despite my poor way of handling the situation, it didn't cost me my relationship with my dad.

Can communication solve all problems? No. Nor are there any guarantees that if you communicate in a good way your parents will do the same. However, one fact remains: Good communication will give you the best possible chance to work out your problems with your parents and get what you want.

Sometimes, we have very good reasons for *not* trying to communicate better with our parents. Other times, we avoid doing so because we really don't know *how* to communicate with them.

5. THE SAFETY FACTOR

On a scale of 1 to 10 (with 1 being "not safe at all" and 10 being "very safe"), put a check (✓) on each scale below to represent how safe you feel communicating with your parents. Explain your rating for each parent. Be as specific as possible.

WITH MY DAD:

NOT SAFE AT ALL	1	2	3	4	5	6	7	8	9	10	VERY SAFE

Dad gets a # _____ because _____

_____

_____

WITH MY MOM:

NOT SAFE AT ALL	1	2	3	4	5	6	7	8	9	10	VERY SAFE

Mom gets a # _____ because _____

_____

_____

Parents' Problems

Perhaps your mom and/or dad have some problems that make it difficult for you to talk with them. Some parents have not healed at all from the separation or divorce, or they haven't healed enough to be able to help you. Some parents are consumed by their own hurt and anger. Sometimes parents can't be there for you because they have serious problems or unresolved grief that gets in the way. Sometimes a parent has a mental illness or a problem with substance abuse or addiction and doesn't get help for it. Then there are those parents who never learned how to treat their kids responsibly because their parents didn't treat them properly.

All of these situations can cause parents to act poorly when you try to talk with them. They may take their anger out on you, make excuses, blame someone or something else, lie, deny that there's a problem, or try to change the subject.

Does any of this fit your parent? If so, try the following:

- **Address the roadblock your parent is putting in front of you.**
  For example, if your dad always gets angry with you when you bring up money issues, you could say, "Dad, it seems that any time I try to talk with you about how we're going to pay for my college tuition, you get angry at me. Can you help me understand why this is getting you so upset?"

- **Be direct and clear.**
  It's easy to think that your parent should know what you need without you having to spell it out. But if what you have said is not getting through, you have to work harder to make your communication direct and clear. Make sure your tone isn't nasty or condescending.

- **Know your limits.**

  Ideally, your efforts at communicating constructively will motivate your parent(s) to do the same. However, your parent(s) may still not be able to respond like you'd hoped. If this happens, it might be time to accept that you cannot change your parent and "move on."

Understanding who your parents really are can help you see how the situation got so complicated. It's sort of like an SUV hitting your parents' car, which then rams into the car you're in. If it weren't for the poor driver in the SUV, your parents' car might never have crashed into yours.

Sometimes, parents' failings are not entirely their fault.

This doesn't excuse a parent from being a good parent, but it can help you understand where he or she is coming from. When my dad kept blaming my mom for his shortcomings, I set out to do my own "research project." I asked my mom and aunt about my dad's upbringing, and gradually I began to understand more about him. I found out that my dad's father abandoned him when he was a baby and that my dad's mom had worked very hard to provide for the family but wasn't there for him emotionally. So he grew up as a very hurt kid and later became a very angry man who never healed from this loss.

My dad's troubles didn't excuse him for not being a responsible father. However, finding out these facts helped me understand his limitations and, as a result, the limitations of his love for me.

It can be scary to see your parents' vulnerabilities, since they are the people whose love and guidance you need most. And it can hurt even more because it brings you face-to-face with a loss you can't fix or do anything about. But it's worth a little detective work. What you know and understand about your parents' weaknesses can go a long way toward helping you understand where they're coming from—and letting yourself off the hook as the cause.

6. WHAT'S THE PROBLEM?

How well do you know your parents? List the top 5 weaknesses you've noticed in your parents, especially the things that bug you the most. If there's something about either parent that you don't understand, note that too.

MOM:

1. _____

2. _____

3. _____

4. _____

5. _____

DAD:

1. _____

2. _____

3. _____

4. _____

5. _____

Remember, no matter how cool someone else's parent(s) may seem to you, lots of teens have problems with their parents. After all, none of us is perfect. What's important to keep in mind is that the more you try to work on the problems you're having with your parent(s) the better you will end up feeling about yourself, even if the result isn't quite what you hoped for. Because then you will know you tried your best, and anytime you do that you're sure to be a winner.

7. EXTRA WAYS TO HELP YOURSELF

- Write down the problem(s) you wrote about in your "Dear Parent" letters. Then, imagine this problem from your parent's side. Journal what your parent's thoughts and feelings regarding the problem might be.

- Which of your mom's and dad's weaknesses is hardest for you to accept? Chose one from **"6. What's the Problem?"** and write more about why this is tough for you. Then write about some of the reasons you think your parent behaves this way.

Parents: What Am I Going to Do With Them?

I step into Dad's living room. It feels weird, being alone in his house. *If only the furniture could talk. There's so much I'd like to know.*

I sit down on the couch and try to get comfortable. I have no idea when he'll be back from his appointment. I open my book and start to read, but I can't concentrate.

I look around the living room. Slowly, I try to imagine telling Dad what's really going on with me. How I'd like him to be a bigger part of my life. How scared I am about going away to college. All the questions I have about what to major in.

I hug my legs. *I wish I could ask him for the help I need.*

I hug my legs tighter. *But what if it comes out all wrong, and he thinks less of me? Maybe it will make him uncomfortable. Maybe he couldn't care less about what I need from him.*

I look up at the rectangular window near the ceiling. Rays of bright sunlight poke down from it, forming long diagonal lines. Looking at them, I start to feel a little calmer. *Maybe telling Dad how I feel is the right thing to do.*

Road Blocks

It wasn't until many years after my parents' separation, when I was in college, that I felt ready to talk with them about the divorce and my difficulties with it. Why did it take me so long? Because I kept focusing on all the reasons *not* to talk with them.

My mental list for my dad went something like this:

1) He might reject me for good.
2) I don't want to make him feel any worse.
3) Maybe he doesn't really care about what I have to say.

My list for my mom was:

1) She might get angry and yell at me.
2) She will likely start bad-mouthing Dad.
3) I don't want to make her feel more guilt about the divorce.

1. WHAT'S IN YOUR WAY?

Think about the times you avoid talking with your parents about their separation, divorce or remarriage, and the problems you have with the whole thing. For each parent, jot down some of the things that get in the way of talking with them.

WITH MOM:

1. _____

2. _____

3. _____

4. _____

5. _____

WITH DAD:

1. _____

2. _____

3. _____

4. _____

5. _____

Now, put your reasons aside for a bit and regroup. First, it's important to realize this fact: Even if you have the easiest parents in the world to get along with, talking with them about problems—especially ones they're involved in—still requires courage. Focusing on the good that can result will help you find that courage.

"Why Bother?"

There actually are four benefits of talking with parents about problems:

1) When done thoughtfully, you are really telling your parent, *I love you and want our relationship to be better.* Reassuring your parent of your love is always a good thing.

2) By communicating, you show respect for yourself as well. You have feelings and desires, and they need to be recognized.

3) Communication is probably the only way your relationship with your parent(s) will have a chance to improve. If you do nothing, nothing is likely to change. Maybe the problem will even get worse because your hurt and anger will build and you may feel even more distant.

4) Your parents might not be aware that you're upset. Or your parents may be even more afraid than you are to bring up the problem.

There's another major benefit for you. By trying to work out your problems with your parents, you improve the chances for your own dating relationships to succeed. Otherwise, your problems can quickly turn into baggage that works against you. If you get married someday, that baggage might even influence you to marry someone who is not right for you.

"I'll Show Them!"

There are also some not-so-good reasons for talking with parents about problems. Suppose, for example, you're thinking, *Maybe I can get my parents to change or teach them to be better parents.* If so, stop wishing! This isn't the purpose of confronting them, nor is it healthy to try to "parent" your parents.

You might also see this talk as a way of punishing a parent. If so, let go of it. Attempting to punish a parent will only worsen the problem. Plus, justice is always best left with God.

It may be a bit of a stretch for you to imagine something good coming out of talking with your parent(s). If so, try imagining the communication "glass" as half-full—that each step toward better communication matters. If you see the glass as half-empty—in other words, that nothing will help the situation—that's likely what will happen. Give yourself a chance to think positively.

2. HALF-FULL OR HALF-EMPTY?

Describe in detail at least one good outcome that might result from talking with your parent(s).

"Off Limits!"

You might be avoiding communicating with your parent(s) for another reason, one you might not even realize: You may have weak boundaries. This means having difficulty saying "no" when you need to. When you set a boundary, you create your personal property line, a limit that shows where you end and another begins. It's how to show respect for yourself.

Consider your room, for example. You know where it begins and ends. You're responsible for cleaning up your own mess, but you're not responsible for making the bed or picking up clothes in another person's bedroom, right? That's the other person's responsibility. Similarly, that person is not responsible for cleaning up your room.

Inside your room is also where you keep things you like and keep out what you don't like. Boundaries work the same way. They help you keep the good stuff in and the bad stuff out.

3. BORDER CHECKPOINT

How solid are your boundaries with each of your parents? Check (✓) the statements that describe your relationship with either parent.

WITH DAD: **WITH MOM:**

❐   ❐   I sometimes give in because it's easier.

❐   ❐   I often say "yes" when I really want to say "no."

❐   ❐   I try to avoid conflict at all costs.

❐   ❐   I often feel manipulated.

❐   ❐   I sometimes don't speak up about how I really feel or what I really think.

❐   ❐   I'm a good person. Sometimes, I feel like they take advantage of me because of it.

❐   ❐   They don't take me seriously very often.

❐   ❐   I often pay more attention to their feelings than my own.

❐   ❐   I usually wait until I get angry before I stand up for myself.

❐   ❐   I'm not really as upbeat as I appear around them.

How many statements did you check? If you checked six or more, your boundaries are a little weak. This can cause your parent not to take you seriously enough. It can also cause your parent to make unfair demands of you, such as:

- Expecting you to become a replacement parent to your younger sibling.
- Encouraging you to take sides against your other parent.
- Asking you to deliver messages to your other parent.
- Looking to you as a confidante or shoulder to cry on.

While you can't control what your parents do and don't do, you can work on setting and communicating your boundaries with them. You may find that they respect you more as a result.

Communication 101

You may be thinking, *I hardly think I need lessons in communicating. I can talk with my friends just fine!* Here's the thing: The tougher the situation, the harder it is to communicate what you really mean—especially if you don't want to hurt the other person. Communicating effectively is a skill that you will be practicing and improving for the rest of your life.

In their book *Let Love Change Your Life*, counselor Dr. Roger Tirabassi and his wife, Becky, have put together some terrific guidelines for getting across what you really want to say. As you read them, put a plus (+) by the guidelines you already use and a minus (-) by those you might need to work on.

- **Don't use the words "never" and "always."**

  When you are angry or frustrated, it's easy for "never" and "always" to slip out, but they can cause the other person to feel unfairly accused and become defensive. These words are often exaggerations and don't paint an accurate picture.

- **Don't blame, shame or call names.**

  When you feel angry, hurt or frustrated, you may feel like striking back so the other person *feels* what you're feeling. However, striking back ultimately hurts your relationship.

- **Use "I" statements rather than "you" statements.**

  It's much easier for your parent to hear you say, "I'm upset," than to hear you say, "*You* upset me!" "You" statements cause people to feel blamed or accused. They end up defending themselves rather than listening to you. When you use an "I" statement, however, you are taking responsibility for your feelings. Take a look at these examples and think about how you would feel if you were on the receiving end of each:

  "You" Message: "You never have any time for me anymore. All you care about is your boy/girlfriend." Or, "You hardly ever call or see me. It seems like you don't care about me anymore."

  "I" Message: "I feel sad when I don't get to talk with you on a regular basis."

- **Take a time-out.**

  If you are too angry or too disappointed to speak thoughtfully, take a time-out. Otherwise, you may say or do something that will hurt your parent and damage your relationship.

- **Check out what you hear before you respond.**

  Good communication involves trying to understand what the other person thinks or feels about a problem. This will help you get along better and find a solution. Check out what your parent has said by repeating it back in your own words. For example, respond with, "So, what you're saying is…. Is that right?"

- **Don't interrupt.**

  Give your parent a chance to share. Interrupt only if you need to ask a question to understand better what is being said. Remember that you will get a chance to share once your parent is finished.

- **Don't use threats.**

  Threats don't solve problems and can make things worse. If you feel like threatening someone, call for a time-out.

- **Be positive.**

  Thank your parent for talking with you. Even if you disagree, you can still thank your parent for sharing his or her thoughts and feelings. Work to keep your communication positive.

Here are a few more suggestions I would add:

- **Focus on one problem or concern.**

  Good communication isn't a protest session where you bring up everything—past and present—that's bothering you. Instead, calm down and focus on one problem or concern. (You may need to release some of your built-up frustration ahead of time by exercising/playing sports, journaling, or venting to a friend.)

- **If you're really nervous, test the waters first with a less threatening topic.**

  If the thought of talking with your parent about a particular problem is really stressing you out, try discussing a less major issue first, such as your chores. This can build your confidence for addressing a more difficult issue later on. Your parent may need this extra practice as well.

- **Pay attention to your body language.**

  Helpful body language involves making eye contact, facing your parent, and standing an appropriate distance away while talking. When you do these things, you show your parent respect and a good attitude.

- **Avoid using the word "should."**

  "Should" suggests that there's only one right way to do something. It can also make your parent feel as if you're trying to control or attack him or her. As a result, your parent may get defensive and the talk may get completely off track.

- **Choose a time that's good for both of you.**

  If your parent has just gotten home from work or is busy making dinner, it's probably not a great time to begin your talk. Similarly, if your parent is tired or distracted with some other pressing matter, wait for a better time. If you're not sure when a good time might be, ask your parent.

This whole experience of separation and divorce is rough territory, and you deserve to be heard and understood. These communication guidelines can help. The next time you're planning on talking with a parent, run down the list first, so the suggestions are fresh in your mind. Some of them may seem a bit awkward when you first try them, especially if the language is different from what you usually use, but it's worth the effort. You may be surprised by turns in the conversation you didn't expect.

Road Trip

Okay. Now it's time to focus on what you need and want from your parent—and how you are going to communicate it. Your communication plan will work best if it addresses five main parts. Think of them as steps along a road trip, all necessary in order to get to where you want to go. If you overlook one or more steps, your car might break down or you might get lost. So, too, can communication break down if it doesn't have the following five parts to support it.

4. WHAT'S YOUR PLAN?

For each of the steps below, write out what you might say to your parent.

STEP 1: Get your car checked out.

This first step is pretty basic. Before hitting the road, you'll need to know if your car is ready. Do you have enough oil, air in the tires and—most especially—coolant? In communication terms, this means asking yourself this question first: *"Can I talk with my parent without blowing up and trashing the communication guidelines?"*

If your answer is "no," then wait a bit. Otherwise, you're likely to say or do something you regret, which will only make your problem worse.

If your answer is "yes," then ask yourself: *"Have I done anything that has added to the problem (such as hanging up on a parent, insulting or avoiding him or her)?*" If this doesn't apply to you, move on to Step 2. If it does apply, it is important to apologize to your parent for whatever you did or said that hurt him or her before going on to Step 2. For practice, write out your apology here:

EXAMPLE: "Dad, I know I haven't been speaking to you when you've called. I haven't been returning your calls either. I'm sorry about that."

_____

_____

_____

_____

_____

STEP 2: Pack munchies, enough cash, and the right clothes.

Road trips can get dicey if the A/C or heater breaks, or you run into bad weather, or you're stuck in bad traffic. You can make your life easier by anticipating what you might need during your trip.

When communicating with parents, you may not have any idea how they'll respond to a particular problem or what might detour the conversation. What you can be pretty sure of, though, is that they're just as nervous and worried about communicating with you as you are with them. So get your stuff together before you talk. Prepare the way by reminding your parent that you care. If you start with a positive, your parent will have a better chance of hearing about the problem. For practice, write that positive on the next page.

EXAMPLE: "I care about you a lot and want our relationship to be better."

_____

_____

_____

_____

_____

_____

_____

STEP 3: Plan with a map and directions.

Maybe you're the kind of person who would rather wing it. Maybe you assume you can always ask for directions along the way. However, the person you ask might not know the area well enough or may lead you in the wrong direction. And what happens if you run into a detour?

In order to improve your chances for getting where you want to go in your conversation with your parents, you'll need to pinpoint what's causing the problem. In the space below, define the problem you're having with your parent as specifically as you can. Focus on only one problem or behavior.

EXAMPLE: "It really bothers me that you don't make me a priority. I'll give you some examples. Last Thursday, you called and talked the entire time about your girlfriend. Then, on Saturday, you asked me to go hunting, when you know I don't like to hunt."

Or, when setting a boundary: "I want to talk to you about the way you put me in the middle with Dad. For example, the other day you said, 'Tell your dad that I told you to ask him for the money.'"

_____

_____

_____

_____

_____

_____

_____

STEP 4: Take time to notice the scenery.

At this point in the communication, you might feel like speeding through because this step is where you reveal your deeper needs and feelings. This may seem awkward and even scary, especially if you haven't opened up in this way to your parent before. Or maybe your parent has seemed unconcerned about your feelings in the past. In either case, though, this step is really important because it ensures your best chances for being heard.

Communication speed matters when you're online. But not when you're getting to the nitty-gritty about tough issues face-to-face. While you may be tempted to drive as fast as you can to get to your destination, you'll miss the good stuff along the way. If you slow down and take the time to get in touch with how your parent's actions or inactions are really affecting you, and then communicate this as best you can, your parent is likely to pay attention.

In the space below, define how the problem with your parent is affecting you.

Example: "When you call and cancel our time together, I feel like you don't really care about me. It pushes me away from you."

Or, when setting a boundary: "Your comments about Mom really hurt me and push me away from you."

_____

_____

_____

_____

_____

_____

STEP 5: Get out and stretch.

You're almost there. This last part is where you ask your parent specifically for what you want from him or her and the benefit that would result from it. If you are communicating a boundary, note a consequence that you are prepared to act on.

Or if you're not sure what a good solution would be, you can ask your parent for help by saying, "I'm not sure how to fix this. Do you have any ideas?"

Use the space below to write down what you want from your parent.

Example: "I want you to ask about my life and interests. It would help me feel closer to you."

Or when setting a boundary: "I want you to stop putting me in the middle and saying hurtful things like that. If you don't, I'm going to leave the room every time I see you."

_____

_____

_____

_____

_____

_____

At this point, you may be thinking, *This is way too much work! My parents should be doing all this, not me. After all, they're the adults.* If this describes you, remember that one of the goals of communication is to help you get what *you* want. It's also a way to respect and take care of yourself because, by communicating, you're establishing yourself as a separate, valuable person who needs to be taken seriously. While you can't control how your parents treat you, you can control how you *allow* them to treat you. If you avoid talking to your parent about a problem, you're actually allowing it to happen!

Where the Rubber Meets the Road

There's one more important reason for working on improving communication with your parents: It shows your parents that you honor them.

Somewhere along the line, you've probably heard the Fourth Commandment: "Honor your father and your mother." But just about now, you may be wondering how this commandment applies to your parents—especially if they're treating themselves, or each other, or you poorly.

First, it's important to know that honoring does not mean obeying without questioning. Nor does it mean you need to excuse your parents' behavior. You can hold them accountable and still address your parents with consideration, no matter what they have done.

Here are some specific examples of how you can apply this commandment to parents who have really failed you:

- Don't cut off contact with them.
- Acknowledge that they're not perfect.
- Don't talk down to them or shout at them.
- Pray for them.
- Ask someone else for help if one of your parents is struggling with abuse or alcohol or drug problems.
- Try to forgive and, when possible, reconcile with them.
- Be appreciative for what they have given you (including the gift of life).

Honoring your parents may be difficult—perhaps even the most difficult challenge you will ever face. However, in addition to being commanded by

God, honoring your parents is important because it shows how you honor others. You will always be running into difficult people and situations in your life, and your relationship with your parents is a practice ground for future relationships. And remember: No matter what, God sees your efforts and will honor you for them.

5. EXTRA WAYS TO HELP YOURSELF

- Put your communication plan into practice. You can do this by reviewing the statements you wrote in this chapter and then (1) saying them to your parent in person or (2) writing them to your parent in an e-mail or letter. Then, share what happens with a trusted friend.
- Ask yourself how you can do a better job of honoring your parents. Try out at least two different things this week that you don't normally do.

Family:
Will I Ever Have One Again?

Steve plants both his elbows on the TV tray and clutches his hands into a fist. He looks down every few minutes from the football game to his sheets of statistics. His sister, Mary, pokes her head in.

"Can you get me a cup of coffee?" he asks, then looks back at the TV.

"Yeah, sure." Mary frowns, then leaves.

Steve knows there must be something she wants to talk about. The last thing his sister likes to do is watch sports.

Mary returns with a cup of coffee and sets it on the end table, away from his papers.

"The Ravens just scored another touchdown," he says. "There's no way the Steelers will catch up now."

"They play so many games. What's it matter if they lose?"

Steve raises his eyebrows at her. "Don't you have something to do?" he asks, half joking, half serious.

"*You're* something," Mary throws in before leaving.

The Ravens win. Steve jumps up, clapping and yelling.

Mary comes back, shaking her head.

"Now, that's what I call a good victory," Steve says, tossing his pen on the TV tray.

"Any other games on?" Mary sits down in the recliner chair.

Steve continues paging through his statistics. "Not till tomorrow night."

"Steve, there's something I want to ask you."

"Yeah, go ahead." He jots down another figure.

Mary takes a deep breath and clasps her hands. "Looks like Mom wants us to meet her new boyfriend."

Steve shrugs his shoulders. *So what?* he thinks. *Mom doesn't really care about me. Why should I bother meeting her boyfriend?*

Mary sits up. "She's invited us to dinner with them. I think we should go."

Steve glares at her. "I have better things to do."

"You know, Mom sounds a lot happier now. Maybe she'll start doing more things with us. I know it'll be different with this guy in the picture, but maybe we can be more like a family."

Steve grabs hold of the arms of his chair. "We don't have a family anymore, and we never will." He looks back at the TV and cracks his knuckles.

"I can't believe you're saying that!"

Steve continues to look away from her. He wishes he could have a normal family like his friends.

"Look, I know Mom hasn't treated you right, but maybe things will be better now."

Steve turns toward Mary. "Would you just get on with your life," he says slowly and calmly. He stares at her until she looks away. Then he looks back at the TV. All he can think about is how much his family isn't a family anymore. And now he and Mary will probably be replaced for good.

After a few minutes he asks, "What, is she planning to marry him or something?"

"I don't know. Probably. At least she cares enough to have us meet him."

"I don't know why you always get your hopes up. You'll only get disappointed again."

"It could be a lot worse, you know. She could have moved away and never seen us again."

Steve switches the channels. He knows that's true, but it still didn't make them a family.

"The dinner reservations are for eight o'clock Friday at Michael's. That's this coming Friday."

"At least she picked a decent place to eat."

"You need to give people a second chance, Steve. It'll make your life a lot better."

"I love Mom, but I don't *like* her. Her boyfriend isn't going to change that. Nothing will. Can't you get that through your head?"

Mary storms out the room and slams the door.

Family Breakups

Once my dad left home, I felt as if I didn't have a family anymore. His leaving broke up more than my mom and dad's marriage. It broke us up as a family, like a cue ball hitting a rack of balls in a game of pool. We all hurt so much, and that made it tough to be there for one another. My mother, brothers and I often handled our hurts alone. My mom would cry by herself in her bedroom.

One of my brothers would go out and race his car, while my other brother played sports. And I would either listen to music, talk to my dog, or bury myself in homework. We stopped doing things together as a family, too, like going on vacations. I thought we'd never be a real family again.

1. THE ROUGH ROAD

Below are some ways in which families can change after a separation or divorce. Check (✓) the ones that describe your family. When you're finished, go back and put a star (*) by the change that's toughest for you.

_____ We moved to a new house. I live in two different homes.

_____ I have less time with one or both of my parents.

_____ My parents are not like themselves anymore. Examples: Mom/Dad is always crying, yelling or doing something destructive like abusing drugs or alcohol.

_____ We don't do things as a family anymore .

_____ We have less money. I can't get as many clothes or go out with friends as much.

_____ One (or both) of my parents has started dating or has remarried.

_____ My parents are putting me in the middle of their fights.

_____ My mom no longer uses her married name so we have different last names.

_____ The parent I'm living with works longer hours or has gone back to school.

_____ I have to do more chores now.

_____ I had to get a job.

_____ I'm told nothing. My parents keep secrets or never give me a
straight answer.

_____ Other: _____

_____

_____

_____

_____

Family Ties

Whenever there's a loss, family members either draw closer together or grow more distant. My parents' separation brought me and my older brother, Marc, a lot closer. We talked often about the changes and shared our feelings about our parents. It was a great comfort having Marc there to lean on and guide me. It made me feel a lot less alone. He became very protective of me, which made my dad's absence less scary.

Maybe you, too, feel more responsible now for looking after a younger sibling or even a parent who might be having a hard time with the separation or divorce. Perhaps you see your grandparents or other relatives more often now as well. Give yourself a few minutes to consider those in your family to whom you are closest these days.

2. GROWING CLOSER

Has your parents' separation or divorce brought you closer to any family members? If so, explain. (Note: This can include stepparents or stepsiblings, but focus on your biological family first.)

_____

_____

_____

_____

_____

_____

Out of Sync

Separation and divorce may not take away your family, but it can make it a lot harder to *be* one. Maybe your parents are making it difficult because they keep fighting, even in front of you. Or perhaps, as in the opening story, you are more or less resigned to your parent's "bad behavior."

I was always sympathetic toward my dad's actions but critical of my mom's mistakes. It was as if my dad couldn't do anything wrong, while my mom couldn't do anything right. This caused a lot of arguments between me and my mom. I also missed my dad a lot and was confused about why he wasn't more involved in my life. This, too, caused disagreements with my mom. Sometimes I'd ask her about him and this got her angry, because she was still so upset with him. She also feared that my dad would hurt me like he had hurt her. She didn't communicate this to me at the time, though. Instead, she told me to "get over it," as if my dad were like an old boyfriend. I didn't feel as though my mom and I would ever see eye-to-eye about my dad.

3. GAP ASSESSMENT

Has the separation or divorce pushed you away from any family members? If so, explain. (Note: This can include stepparents or stepsiblings, but focus on your biological family first.)

_____

_____

_____

_____

_____

Being There

I wanted to help my family members feel better, but I didn't know how. I eventually learned that one of the best ways to help them was simply to *be* there for them. Some nights my mother and I would listen to music, especially soft, slow, peaceful songs. We didn't talk, but simply sat together in the living room and listened. Other times, I would bake cookies for my brother Marc after school or spend extra time listening to him talk about Dad.

Here are some ways to be there for family members:

- When they are expressing their feelings, don't change the subject or try to fix things. Instead, just listen with your heart.
- Remind them that you care by saying, "I love you," hugging them, or sending them a card or e-mail.
- Invite a family member to go to a movie, the mall, or a sporting event with you.
- Ask a family member how you can help him or her.

What also helped me be there for my family was trying to stand in their shoes and understand what they were going through. This meant thinking about what they had lost because of the separation or divorce and the added struggles they now had.

4. STANDING IN THEIR SHOES

List the names of your family members. Beside each name, note what struggle(s) he or she may be experiencing as a result of the separation or divorce.

EXAMPLES:

My mom: Has less money to pay bills, and it's stressing her out.

My dad: Is really lonely now that he's living by himself.

FAMILY MEMBER	STRUGGLE(S) SINCE THE SEPARATION/DIVORCE
_____	_____
_____	_____
_____	_____
_____	_____
_____	_____
_____	_____

What was most difficult for me was knowing that people in my family were grieving and that I couldn't take the hurt away. For a long time, I fooled myself into thinking I could. I thought being the person my mother wanted me to be would erase all her pain from the divorce. I also tried to talk my brothers out of feeling sad or angry by repeating what I had heard in church about forgiveness. While I had good intentions, I needed to realize that all family members had to work through their own grief. I couldn't do it for them.

It's important to recognize that, while your family members are struggling with grief just as you are, they may be in a completely different grief stage. (See Chapter 1 for a refresher on the stages of grief.) This can make your family feel even less like a family. In the opening story, Steve thought only the worst, while Mary had wishful thoughts. This reflected the different stages of grief they were experiencing: Steve was in the anger stage, while Mary was in denial. Family members need to move through grief in their own way and at their own rate.

A separation or divorce ultimately shows us loud and clear that our family isn't perfect. This can make us think that families without separated or divorced parents must be normal. It's important to understand, though, that *all* families have problems and experience loss. Some families experience illness or death. Some parents lose their jobs. Other families have their houses destroyed by fires or floods. Some teens don't live with their biological parents. There's no such thing as a perfect family, because none of us is perfect to begin with.

Nevertheless, this doesn't change the importance of trying to love and support family members as best you can. This is especially important when you are part of a Christian family, because that means you are part of a community of faith, hope and love.

"It's Not Just 'Us' Anymore"

I had a really hard time when my mom started dating. All I kept thinking was, *Now I'm going to lose Mom just like I'm losing Dad.* Truth was, I was terrified.

Once I went away to college, though, I felt differently. I actually wanted my mom to date because then she would have someone there to care for her, especially when I was living far away. I realized, too, that dating could bring her happiness which, in turn, could positively impact all areas of her life. Finding someone special gave my mom more—not less—love to give. I had it wrong when I was younger. I had thought that if my mom cared for someone else, she would have less love for me.

I didn't understand that the love my mom had for me was different from any other kind of love. I didn't have to compete for it, nor would it fade if she found someone else who was important to her. While it was true that her boyfriend would take up some of her time, that could never take away her love for me.

If your parent is dating or has remarried, you might feel as if you're losing your family even more. It's normal to feel awkward about this new person. After all, he or she is causing changes to your family all over again. You might have your guard up even more because you want to be sure this new person won't hurt your parent. All of this is normal. Just as in any relationship, it will take time to get to know and trust this new person in your parent's life. Take things slowly.

Years after my parents separated, my mom found a serious boyfriend. Even though my dad was living across country, I felt as if I was being disloyal to him by liking my mom's boyfriend. The same was true with my dad's girlfriends.

Maybe you're in a similar situation. Maybe you're not quite sure if it's okay to hug your stepdad or to invite your stepmom (and not your mom) to go somewhere with you. Or maybe one parent puts pressure on you or tells you things so you *won't* like your other parent's boyfriend, girlfriend or spouse. Here are a few things to keep in mind:

- Accepting your parent's relationship with someone new isn't wrong. Instead, it's part of growing up and enduring changes in life.

- Being nice to this new person doesn't mean you're replacing your parent. That isn't possible. Nor does having a friendly relationship with this new person mean that you love your parent any less. Instead, by trying to accept this new person you are trying to get along with everyone.

- If your parents are divorced or in the process of getting a divorce, your mom no longer belongs to your dad, and he no longer belongs to her. By finding new partners and new happiness, your parents are trying to move on with their lives.

- If you find yourself saying "No!" to this new person, no matter what, it could be that you're really saying "No" to what this person represents: the fact that your parents aren't going to get back together. Dig deeper to see if this is the real issue. It's unfair to take your disappointment out on a new person in your parent's life.

- Give yourself a break. You don't need to do anything more initially than recognize that this new person is someone your parent enjoys being with. And you don't need to do anything more than be polite to him or her.

- Don't pressure yourself to feel a certain way. If you develop a relationship with the new person, that's an added bonus. However, it might never happen. Let the relationship evolve in its own time.

5. STICKY SITUATIONS

Has either of your parents started dating or gotten remarried? Has this resulted in new problems or concerns for you? If so, write (or draw) about them below.

6. STICKY SITUATIONS REVISITED

Now, put those problems or concerns aside and look at the situation from your parent's point of view. Has your parent gained anything positive from this relationship? Or has it been all negative? Write (or draw) your response below.

Ties that Bind

In my family, it took years for each of us to accept the losses caused by the divorce. However, despite our struggles, good things resulted. I learned just how important it was to be there for my family members in their times of need. I also became more appreciative of the love and support I received from them. I began to admire my family members, because I knew firsthand just how much courage and strength it took to accept the losses and grow from them.

I no longer take my family for granted. My family is still very much a family, even though it has changed.

Take a few minutes to think about your own family as it is at this time.

7. RELATIONSHIPS OF THE HEART

In what ways is your family still a family? Or, if you can't think of anything, explain why you feel you don't have a family anymore.

_____

_____

_____

_____

_____

_____

_____

_____

Focusing on the good things about the changes in your family may not be easy, nor is reaching out to your family members. However, one thing is for sure: The more you try, the more you will feel like a family again. You will also find that instead of being something that divides you, your parents' breakup can become something that draws you closer together.

8. EXTRA WAYS TO HELP YOURSELF

- Do something nice for a family member with whom you don't get along well or aren't very close to. If you're not sure what to do, ask that person how you can help him or her.

- Suggest that your family do a family activity once a month. Consider doing something fun together or having a family meeting where you discuss holiday or vacation plans and/or any conflicts you're having.

- Share your response to **"5. Sticky Situations"** with your parent, either in person, on the phone, or via email. You may want to refer to **"4. What's Your Plan?"** in Chapter 5 for extra guidance.

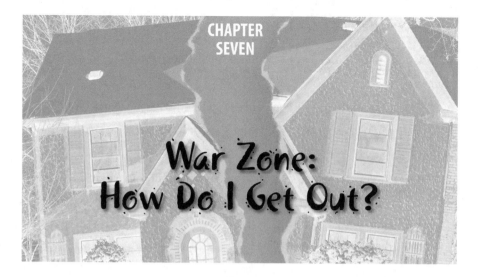

CHAPTER SEVEN

War Zone:
How Do I Get Out?

John turns away from the door and cups his hand over the phone. "I'd like to stay another week or so, Mom."

"Another *week*? You've already been there two weeks. That's a lot longer than we agreed on." She goes on to list all the projects she needs him to do at home: mow the lawn, clean the basement, sort through his old clothes for Goodwill to pick up.

"I know," John says, "but I'm really having fun. Dad has a boat, and he's teaching me how to water ski." He wants to mention that he's getting to know his dad better, but instead adds, "I'm getting pretty good."

"Is he still living with Roxanne, or has he found another bimbo? She's young enough to be your sister, you know."

John shakes his head. *Here it comes again*, he thinks. He agrees that it's wrong for his dad to be living with a woman he's not married to, but why should John be punished because of it? "She's not a bad person, Mom," he finally says.

"So, he *is* still living with her. That man should rot...."

Said the wrong thing again, John thinks. *Won't I ever learn to keep my mouth shut?*

"You know, Julie hasn't been able to get her grades because your father still hasn't paid the tuition bill. I bet he's spending a good bit on that tramp, though."

John remembers his father's advice: If your mother gives you any flack, tell her to get a life; you're old enough to make your own decisions. "I should be able to stay longer if I want to," John says.

"Go ahead and continue to treat him like a king, after all he's done to us."

"John," his father calls, "dinner's ready."

"Mom, I've got to go. I'll call you tomorrow."

A click sounds on the other end, then a dial tone.

John hangs up the phone, feeling like the most selfish person in the world…and the most confused.

Caught in the Middle

You probably know what it feels like to be caught in the middle of your parents' battles. It's as if you've landed in a War Zone, a high conflict area between your parents. When this happens, all kinds of bad stuff gets thrown at you, either intentionally or unintentionally, because your parents are still upset about the separation or divorce and haven't learned a better way to handle their feelings. You may feel as if they're playing a game of paintball and you're the target. The difference, though, is that this is no fun. In fact, being in the War Zone can really stress you out. How do you typically handle these situations?

1. ENTER THE WAR ZONE

For each example below, circle the letter of the response that you are most likely to make:

1) **If I were John in the story, I'd:**

   a. tell Mom, "Chill out and get a grip!"

   b. probably do what Mom wanted. It's only fair. After all, she's the one raising me.

   c. try to ignore it. It's too much to deal with.

   d. tell Mom that the money problems are not my responsibility, and that I have a right to a relationship with my father.

2) **When my parents put me in the middle of their arguing, I:**

   a. get so angry that we have a shouting match.

   b. am never sure who's really right, so I side with the parent who's having a tougher time with the breakup.

   c. try to avoid the situation.

   d. tell them they're being unfair and to leave me out of it.

3) **When I'm put in the War Zone, I often think:**

   a. my parents are completely clueless.

   b. I must be getting punished for doing something wrong.

   c. just ignore it.

   d. don't take it personally. This often happens when parents break up. The situation is tough for everyone.

4) The best way to handle the War Zone is to:

   a. be as aggressive as I can. It's the best way to prevent the situation from getting worse.

   b. try and please the parent I'm with. If I can get my parent in a better mood, maybe he or she will stop putting me in the middle.

   c. try and escape by going to my room or a friend's house. Watching TV or listening to music helps, too.

   d. try and stay objective, then confront the parent who's putting me in the War Zone as respectfully as I can.

Now, count up the number of times you circled each letter and note it below. This will give you a pretty good idea of how you handle the War Zone. Check out where you stand:

Number of a's _____

Number of b's _____

Number of c's _____

Number of d's _____

THE ATTACKER: If you circled mostly a's, the War Zone gets you so angry that you lash out at your parent(s), siblings or friends. You might even take sides and join in your parent's anger. While it's normal to feel angry, dumping it on others never solves anything. When you react this way, it may help you feel in control, but it pushes people away.

It's time to stop using others as your punching bag. You need to explore constructive ways to get your anger out, so you'll be able to work toward a solution. (See Chapter 8 on anger for more direction.)

THE PLEASER: If you circled mostly b's, you put others' feelings first while ignoring your own. Maybe you feel guilty about how you feel, or you fear getting punished if you speak your mind. Or perhaps you can't stand seeing your parents hurting, so you cover up your feelings and try to cheer them up instead, or play the peacemaker. You might even be blaming yourself, thinking, *I could have prevented all this if I were a better kid.*

While you have good intentions, you need to stick up for yourself and realize that it's your parents' job—not yours—to settle their problems. Their arguments are *theirs*. You also need to find a safe place where you can express your feelings and be heard. Otherwise, your bottled-up feelings can snowball into bigger problems. Finally, reassure yourself that you have a right to love both your parents.

THE AVOIDER: If you circled mostly c's, you try to avoid conflict at all costs. Perhaps you think that the problem will magically go away. Or maybe you've tricked yourself into thinking that someone else will solve it for you. In the meantime, you stay away from the house as much as possible to avoid your parent(s).

It's time to face that there's no easy way out. Avoiding your parents will not solve anything. Instead, it can lead to worse problems. There are many things you can do to help yourself, such as talk straight to your parent about the problem. (See Chapter 5, "Parents: What Am I Going to Do with Them?" for more direction.) Or you might find it helpful to journal or draw your feelings about the War Zone, so you can understand more about what makes it stressful for you. Talking with a school counselor or another trusted adult can be supportive as well.

THE BALANCER: If you circled mostly d's, you do a good job of evaluating the War Zone with fairness and self-control. You don't let your emotions rule you. You stay in touch with who you are and what you want, which also serves you well. And when you stick up for yourself, you do so openly and respectfully—always the best approach for solving conflicts. Congratulations!

Battle Tactics

Because my dad moved out of state and never fought for custody of me, I was kept out of the War Zone somewhat. However, my parents still bad-mouthed each other and tried to get me to take sides. Maybe your parents bad-mouth each other, too, or ask you to deliver messages because they don't want to talk with each other. Or perhaps your parents put you in the War Zone in more subtle ways, such as by bribing you with money, fun vacations, or clothes to gain your loyalty, or by telling you about ongoing problems with your other parent.

2. STUCK IN THE MIDDLE

How do your parents typically put you in the War Zone? Circle all the answers that apply. Then, check (✓) if your mom, dad, or both does it.

WHAT MY PARENTS DO:	WHO DOES IT:	
a. Ask me to be a messenger and/or spy (for example, tell me to ask the other about money, get information on dates, etc.).	❒ Mom	❒ Dad
b. Bad-mouth the other (for example, say negative things about the other parent).	❒ Mom	❒ Dad

c. Scream or curse at the other in front of me.   ❐ Mom   ❐ Dad

d. Force me to choose one parent over the other (for example, saying things like, "If you want me to go to your game, you better not invite your mother; otherwise I won't go" or "I know you'd rather live with me, right? So, why don't you tell your father that?").   ❐ Mom   ❐ Dad

e. Use guilt trips and/or threats (for example, saying things like, "You treat your father like a king after all he's done to us? Maybe I should see you just once or twice a year, like he does!").   ❐ Mom   ❐ Dad

f. Put me down (for example, "Why don't you say something to your mother? Don't you have the guts?").   ❐ Mom   ❐ Dad

g. Act more needy than the other parent or ask for too much help or comfort.   ❐ Mom   ❐ Dad

h. Buy me gifts or take me places in order to coax me to side against the other parent.   ❐ Mom   ❐ Dad

Defense Strategies

When my parents bad-mouthed each other, I always felt very uncomfortable. Sometimes they even told me intimate details about the problems in their marriage. I wanted to shout, *Stop it already! It's so wrong for you to put me in the middle like this. Go pick on someone else!* However, I didn't communicate my feelings effectively with either parent.

Instead, I yelled at my mom fairly often, which led to shouting matches.

With my dad, I stayed quiet and listened. While this helped some, it wasn't enough to stop his bad-mouthing of my mother.

What about you? What do you do to protect yourself?

3. WAR ZONE REVISITED

Think about a time when your parent(s) put you in the War Zone. Write down how you felt and how you responded.

_____

_____

_____

_____

_____

_____

_____

_____

_____

Get Real

It's difficult to know what to do when trapped in the War Zone. Not only may your parents be treating you unfairly, but you also may be treating yourself unfairly by holding on to thoughts and beliefs that aren't accurate.

It can be helpful to remind yourself of what you can—and can't do—about the situation.

4. REALITY CHECK

Below is a list of important facts. Check (✓) those you need to remember.

_____ I don't have the power to fix Mom and Dad's problems or make them happy; only they do.

_____ Refusing to stay in the War Zone won't cost me my relationship with Mom or Dad.

_____ No matter how good my intentions are, when I stay in the War Zone, the only person I'm hurting is me.

_____ In doing what's good and loving for myself, I'm also doing what's good and loving for Mom and Dad.

_____ I shouldn't be afraid to follow my own judgments just because I'm not an adult yet. Teenagers can be right, too. (Parents don't always know or do what's best anyway.)

_____ My job right now is to figure out who I am. This sometimes means separating myself from my parents so I can decide my values, goals and dreams, along with what God wants for me.

Behind Enemy Lines

If it seems as if war is raging around you, it can be helpful to go "behind enemy lines" to see things from the other side. Your parents probably have a lot of hurt and anger about the separation or divorce, just as you do. Maybe one of your parents was unfaithful to the other or wouldn't get help for a problem, like depression or alcoholism. Maybe one or both of them feels betrayed or abandoned. Parents also often fight after their breakup. Sometimes they battle over money, visitation, custody or other matters that can take months, if not years, to resolve.

All of this fighting can bring out the worst in parents. They may become like two sharks who keep using angry weapons—their teeth—to catch and kill prey and tear off lumps of flesh. Sometimes their anger takes on a life of its own, devouring not only them but everything around them—including you. Your parents may get consumed by a desire for revenge against the other, or they may fear feeling the pain of their own problems. As a result, they may try to influence you to take sides and help them.

Your parents may not even realize that they're putting you in the War Zone or just how much they're doing it. It can seem as if they have an unlimited supply of angry weapons. This, too, is like sharks: They lose their teeth during feeding, then grow them back.

In addition, parents often feel guilty about the separation or divorce. They know it makes life more difficult for you, and they sometimes blame themselves for your hurt. To rid themselves of the guilt, they may tell you details about their marital problems because they feel the need to defend their position. Or they might bad-mouth your other parent because they fear that parent will only let you down.

Understanding your parents' sides won't make the War Zone go away. However, it may help you take your parents' actions less personally.

5. GET UNDER THEIR SKIN

Try to put yourself in the "shark's skin" of each of your parents. Write (or draw) what you think might be causing each parent's hurt or anger.

What to Do Next

Now that you have a better understanding of the War Zone, you're better pre-pared to take action against getting caught there. Here are some suggestions that may help you:

• **Respond initially with silence; then correct your parent.**

When my dad bad-mouthed my mom, I stayed quiet. It was my way of say-ing, "I refuse to participate." This encouraged him to stop and consider what he was doing. Often, he would then say to me, "I probably shouldn't be tell-ing you all this." Sometimes, he even changed the subject to my mom's good qualities. (If you like this idea but don't think you can sit there and "zip your lip," try leaving the room and chilling for a while.)

Whether you say nothing or leave the room, follow this up with a state-ment at some point that "corrects" your parent (for example, "It's not fair to put me in the middle" or "I'm not a spy/messenger" or "That's a problem for you and Mom/Dad to work out"). This way, your parent clearly gets the mes-sage that you don't want to be involved.

• **Assert your right to love your parent.**

When my mom bad-mouthed my dad, I sometimes told her, "I have a right to love my father. And nothing you say is going to change that." This not only silenced her but it also helped me stick up for myself.

Remember, you have just one father and mother. You have a right to love them both. It's what God wants for you as well.

• **Ask God for help.**

When my parents put me in the War Zone, I felt confused, guilty and angry. Both my mom and dad wanted me to take sides, but I couldn't. I knew neither one was all right or all wrong. I wanted to please them both, but didn't know how. I also felt angry because I knew their pressure tactics were wrong.

Talking with God helped me get some perspective—and stop feeling that it was my responsibility to fix their problems. It also helped me find the right direction, because I focused on what I believed God wanted me to do.

• **Don't let yourself be manipulated.** Stand your ground and leave the problem in your parent's hands, where it belongs.

For example, suppose one parent says, "If your mom goes to your baseball game, I don't" or "You're going to invite your dad to your recital after all he's done to us?" Realize these are attempts to control you. Don't let yourself be controlled by caving into guilt and inviting only one parent to an event. Doing so rewards your parent(s) for bad behavior.

Let your parents take responsibility for their own decisions and actions. If your dad doesn't go to your game because your mom will be there, then *he* is the one who is responsible for that decision, not you. And if your mom tries to lay on a guilt trip on you instead of respecting your right to have a relationship with your dad, then *she's* the one who's in the wrong.

• **Write your parent(s) a letter.** Spell out how his or her actions upset you. Here's one sample that might give you some ideas of how to word what you want to say:

Dear Dad and Mom,

Ever since the separation, I have tried extra hard to have a good relationship with each of you.

I love you both. However, I now feel llike I have to "choose sides" because of all your bad-mouthing.

I shouldn't have to hear the details of your marital problems or bear the brunt of your anger. When you put down each other, you put me down, too, because I'm part of you both. It really hurts.

I'm starting to lose respect for you. You're both adults and should know better. This is your separation, not mine.

From now on, I'm going to leave the room if you start bad-mouthing. I don't want my relationship with either of you to get ruined, but I need you to help me by not bad-mouthing. This would show me that you really do love me.

Love,

• **Ask a family friend or relative (who hasn't taken sides) to help you.**

This person could take you back and forth to see each parent, or he or she could sit down with all of you and discuss how much the War Zone upsets you.

• **Ask your parents to talk with a family counselor.**

If your parents don't agree to this, ask to see a counselor yourself or talk about the situation with an adult whom you trust (for example, a church pastor, teacher, guidance counselor, coach, etc.)

• **Try to change the subject while staying positive.**

For example, when your mom starts to bad-mouth your dad, you could say, "You know, Mom, I don't see you as much as I did before. Let's not let Dad interfere in our relationship. Our time is too important. By the way, did I tell you I made the basketball team?"

If the action step you choose doesn't seem to help, try another one. Eventually, you will find the one that works for you. What's most important is to keep on trying. Only by taking action can you put an end to being placed in the War Zone. Good luck!

6. EXTRA WAYS TO HELP YOURSELF

- Follow one or more of the action steps from the "What to Do Next" section above. Then note how it worked for you.

- Choose a fact from **"4. Reality Check"** and write a response to it.

Anger: How Do I Get Past It?

The phone rings. Paul checks Caller ID and scrunches his eyebrows, trying to decide whether or not to answer.

It keeps ringing. Paul frowns, then quickly picks up the receiver. "Hello."

"Paul, it's your father," the man on the other end of the line says.

Paul doesn't respond.

"It's been a while since we've talked. How's everything going there?"

"Fine," he says slowly, deliberately calm. *What does his father want?*

"So, how old are you now, eighteen?"

"Seventeen." *Why is he wasting my time?*

"You're probably graduating soon then, aren't you?"

"Not till next year. I'll be a senior in the fall."

"Wow, the years really have flown by."

His father asks him if he's looked into any colleges yet and what he plans to study. The questions roll on. Paul bites his lower lip. He doesn't like this quick way his father is trying to work back into his life.

"So, how are things with you?" Paul asks, wanting to cut to the chase.

"Well, not so good."

Paul nods his head. *Figures. Dad only calls when he needs something.* Then Paul forces out, "What's going on?"

"Well, Ellen, my wife, moved out last week. She's heading out West with her things now as we speak."

Paul rolls his eyes as his father continues to tell him about the arguments leading up to Ellen's leaving. Paul shakes his head as his father talks. *What makes him think I want to hear about this? Is he totally clueless?*

"I think this is all providential, really. I know I haven't been much of a father to you."

This is a bunch of BS, Paul thinks, forcing himself to keep quiet.

"There's a lot I need to explain," his father adds in a serious voice.

Paul feels his insides giving way. *Maybe there are some things Mom hasn't told me about him.* But then he catches himself. *It doesn't matter. I'm not making excuses for him. Nothing can make what he did any less wrong.*

"That's the reason for my call," his father goes on, "but I don't want to get into it all now. There are some things I want to discuss with you in person. I'm coming to San Diego in three weeks for a legal conference. I'll arrive Friday the twenty-third."

"Of June? You mean next week?"

"Yeah. So, I was thinking, if you're not doing anything, maybe we could grab some dinner, say around eight o'clock?"

"That should be okay," Paul says matter-of-factly. His heart is beating so fast, it feels as if it's about to burst out of his chest. He starts pacing.

"I could pick you up, but that'd probably only cause problems with your mother. Could you meet me?"

"I guess so," Paul says. *He'd show up, but that didn't mean anything was going to change.*

"How about I call you once I get settled in, and we can decide on a place. How's that sound?"

"No problem," Paul says.

"Good. Well, I better get back to paying these bills so I can get them in the mail."

"Okay. Thanks for calling," Paul adds, trying to be polite, as if he'd just heard from some college recruiter. "Bye."

"Bye, I love you."

Paul hangs up the telephone, pretending he didn't hear his father's last words. He hits the review button on Caller ID to make sure he's got his dad's number in case he decides to cancel.

"I'm So Mad I Could…"

It's normal to get angry about the fallout from your parents' separation or divorce. Anger is a natural response to hurt, fear, or not getting your way. For instance, maybe your parent promised to go to your game or help you get ready for your homecoming dance, and then didn't show because he or she decided to be with someone else. Or maybe the divorce has heaped too much responsibility on you, and you're getting discouraged about not being able to do what you want. You might even be ticked off because your parents didn't try harder to work out their problems.

Anger, actually, is a good emotion. It protects us and lets us know when we've been hurt or wronged. It also allows us to stand up for ourselves and our beliefs. The problem, though, is that it's easy to overreact with rage, violence, or a hot temper. Or to underreact by stuffing our anger or trying to convince ourselves that we're *not* angry—as Paul did with his father's call. He was fuming because he hadn't heard from his father in a long time and had never gotten an explanation or an apology for it. However, instead of expressing his hurt and anger to his dad, he kept it inside and let it build.

What about you? What do you do with your anger?

1. YOUR "ANGER GRIP"

Check (✓) the things you're likely to do when you're angry.

- ❒ push or hit someone
- ❒ hit or damage things
- ❒ throw things or slam doors
- ❒ pick fights at home, school or when playing sports.
- ❒ tease or mock others
- ❒ yell or scream at those you're angry with
- ❒ insult or threaten others
- ❒ criticize others
- ❒ act sick
- ❒ blame someone else
- ❒ kick or torment a pet
- ❒ drive recklessly

- ❒ talk yourself out of feeling angry
- ❒ feel as if you're being bad or sinful if you get angry
- ❒ feel that someone won't like or love you if you get angry
- ❒ give in to avoid another's anger
- ❒ laugh nervously instead of getting angry
- ❒ ignore whoever upsets you
- ❒ get silent and moody
- ❒ think that God might punish you for being angry

How many checks do you have in the left column?   _____
These are times when you are OVERREACTING.

How many checks do you have in the right column?   _____
These are times when you are UNDERREACTING.

After my parents divorced, I rarely saw or spoke to my dad, so I didn't have many chances to express my anger to him. Even when I did talk with him, I didn't want to waste our time together by being angry. Deep down, I was also afraid that if I expressed my anger, my dad might reject me for good. I also knew he was having difficulty getting his life back together, and I didn't want to make him feel any worse. All these factors encouraged me to keep my anger inside and let it build. Then, I'd explode later, usually taking my anger out on my mom or someone else with whom I felt safe. I always felt worse about myself when that happened, and I hurt my mom in the process.

Take a minute to think about a recent time when you got angry. Did you express it freely? Did you direct it toward the right people, in the right places? Or did you keep your anger inside? And if you did express it, did you do it appropriately or did you make a scene?

2. YOUR "ANGER SCENE"

Write below about a recent time when you got angry. How did you handle the situation? Do you think your action (or inaction) worked for you or against you?

_____

_____

_____

_____

_____

_____

Sorting It Out

As time went on, my father grew more and more distant from me. I was not only hurt but confused. He wasn't the father I thought I knew. It made me question whether I had ever really known him at all. The more I tried to figure him out, the more confused I became. I hated having so many unanswered questions. But I was afraid that if I pushed him for answers my anger would explode and he might reject me for good. Beneath the anger, though, was mostly hurt. I was aching from my dad's neglect.

Maybe you're angry because your parent is making a boyfriend or girl-friend more a priority than you. Or perhaps you're angry at how one of your parents is treating the other. Or you could be angry that you have no say in the changes going on around you, changes that create problems you seem to have no control over.

3. WHAT'S THE REAL DEAL?

Are you angry at your parents? If so, what are you angry at them for? Complete the sentences below.

I'm angry at my dad because: _____

_____

_____

_____

_____

I'm angry at my mom because: _____

_____

_____

_____

_____

Now, rewrite your sentences, this time focusing on your fear or your hurt.

FOR EXAMPLE, if you said, "I'm angry at my dad because he always brings his girlfriend along whenever we do things. And if she doesn't want to do something, I don't get to see my dad," the fear underneath may be, "I'm not as important to my dad as his girlfriend is." Or the underlying hurt may be, "I'm hurt because my dad's girlfriend seems to mean more to him than I do."

With my dad, I fear or am hurt by: _____

_____

_____

_____

_____

_____

With my mom, I fear or am hurt by: _____

_____

_____

_____

_____

_____

Warning Signs

I did a pretty good job of not showing my anger to my dad, but that didn't make it go away. In fact, it made things worse, because my anger came out in destructive ways. I took it out on my mom at times by being overly critical of her and argumentative. This got her angry and hurt her feelings, which pushed us away from each other. I pushed away my friends, too, because I was so competitive in school.

Anger is one determined emotion! If you try to push it away, it only comes back in some other form or place. Since anger is going to come out whether you want it to or not, you need to take charge. Take control of your anger before it takes control of you.

The first step is to pay attention to the signs that warn you when you're getting angry. Your heart may pound faster or your mouth may get dry. Maybe you talk louder or start throwing out insults. Perhaps you clench your fists or breathe faster. Maybe you start pacing.

Treat these signs as a red light that tells you to stop and think. This is your chance to do something constructive—not destructive—with your anger. If you ignore this red light, your anger will only cause you to lose control and you'll likely find yourself in trouble.

4. PROCEED WITH CAUTION

What are the warning signs that signal when you're getting angry?

_____

_____

_____

_____

_____

What Next?

Anger is one of life's trickier emotions because it can be loud and hurtful, or subtle and destructive. But it's important to remember that angry feelings are _not_ wrong or bad. It's what you _do_ when you're angry that can be the problem. Practicing positive ways to express anger is a life-long process.

5. HELP YOURSELF

There are many things you can do to help yourself through anger. Here's a list of some things you might consider. Check (✓) the items that appeal to you.

❐ Replace "hot thoughts" with "cool thoughts" by using positive self-talk. This means telling yourself messages like, "I can handle this. Stop and calm down. Stay in control."

❐ Pound on pillows or clay. Or hit your mattress with a tennis racket or plastic bat. Talk as you hit things.

- ❐ Tear up an old magazine or phone book. Rip each page out and crumble it up; then throw your angry feelings away by throwing the pages in the trash.
- ❐ Find a safe place to scream (or bury your face in a pillow and do so).
- ❐ Jog, exercise, or do some other physical activity.
- ❐ Hit a punching bag.
- ❐ Write about your angry feelings. Or write a letter to the person with whom you are angry (but don't send it).
- ❐ Talk to a friend you trust.
- ❐ Yell into a recorder, play it back, then erase it.
- ❐ Close your eyes and listen. Pay attention to the sounds that are furthest away, then those that are closest to you. Slowly stretch your arms and legs as you open your eyes.
- ❐ Breathe in slowly and deeply while counting to five, then breathe out slowly and deeply to another count of five.
- ❐ Find a deserted spot and shout at God about your feelings.

Now make a promise to yourself to try at least two of the things you checked this week. If these help with your anger, great! If not, try something else next week…and the next and the next. Since managing anger is a life skill, it's important to find what works for you and to keep practicing it so it becomes a strong resource for you.

You're Not Alone

There's one more important thing you can do with your anger: Tell God about your feelings. God knows you're angry. God understands your anger and disappointment better than anyone else. Try putting your feelings into a prayer. It doesn't have to be the kind of prayer you've heard other people say. God can listen to your heart through a song, through writing, through a dance, through a walk of reflection.

The bottom line is that resolving anger is critical to your spiritual health. It can be easy to forget this, especially if you feel your anger is justified. You may be thinking, *I have every right to be angry. I didn't do anything to cause this mess. I'm going to hold on to my anger for as long as I want to.*

Think about what happens when you stay angry at someone. You are basically saying that you no longer care about your relationship with this person. Is that what you really want? Probably not. But it cuts off communication—and kills the possibility of friendship—just the same.

It is similar with God. Holding on to your anger kills your spiritual growth because it closes you off from experiencing the help and support God can give you.

Maybe you're afraid God isn't there, or that God will ask you to do something you don't want to do—like forgive the person with whom you're angry. But the fundamental truth is that God calls us to love. Yes, it is very difficult to love someone with whom you're angry. It may, indeed, be the most difficult challenge of your life. But the important thing to remember is that God doesn't ask you to do this alone.

Give it a try. Talk to God—on your own terms.

6. "GOD, I'VE BEEN THINKING . . ."

Consider someone in your family who is causing you a lot of angry feelings. Imagine sending an e-mail to God about how difficult it is to love this person. Write down what you want to say most.

From:	
To:	God@everywhere.com
Subject:	

7. EXTRA WAYS TO HELP YOURSELF

- Journal your answer to this question: How would your life improve if you handled your anger better?
- Choose one "anger fact" below and journal your response to it.

---

10 ANGER FACTS

1. Anger is a normal response to hurt, frustration or fear.

2. It isn't wrong to get angry. It's what you do when you're angry that can create a problem.

3. You control what you do with your anger. It's a choice that only you can make.

4. Expressing anger from time to time can be good for your health.

5. You can express anger in responsible ways when you stop and think first.

6. Anger drains energy that you could apply toward other goals.

7. The more you take care of your anger, the more at peace you will become.

8. When you stay angry at someone, you give that person control over you.

9. It is wrong for you to be the target of another's anger. It is also wrong for you to use anger to scare and control others.

10. Forgiveness will help you let go of anger.

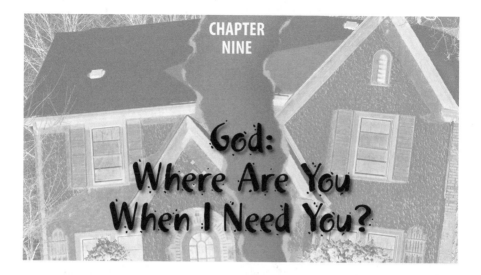

CHAPTER NINE

God: Where Are You When I Need You?

Wearing a long beige robe with a wide band of shiny gold around it, the pastor stands at the podium above everyone. I usually tune out during the sermons, but today he's talking about someone vacationing at the beach and collecting seashells—two of my favorite things—so I listen.

"As the woman was collecting the seashells, it struck her not only how different and individually beautiful each was, but how they all had been lying in the sand, pointed at the ocean. It's the same way with God and the happenings in our lives. Each of us is individually beautiful like a seashell. However, our real beauty, power and strength don't reside in us alone, but in our relationship to God."

I lean back against the pew and think of the last time I was at the beach. It was in February in Florida, and I was fifteen. I remember standing near the ocean and feeling the cool water brush over my bare feet, then the sand tickling underneath as the water retreated. I wasn't thinking about God then, though. I was thinking about my dad and how he was like the waves, moving in and out of my life for the past four years. And I was waiting for the tide to return him for good.

Where is God supposed to fit into this? Knowing how much I need my dad, how could God let this happen? How can God love me yet let me hurt like this?

The pastor continues: "Just as the shells on the beach come from the hand of God, so too are the happenings in our lives connected to God. Some shells are filled with joy and some with pain. Some we might not understand. Still, all are created in relationship to God."

I think of the awesome seashells I have on my bookcase and how perfect they are. Then I think of the broken ones I keep in my desk drawer: an orange starfish with three arms, a silver mussel shell with only one part, a yellow sea horse without its tail. I like all of them too much to throw away, but they don't belong with the others.

I think of the biggest shell on my shelf and how God created it. It's so big it covers my ear when I listen to the ocean sound inside. It's my favorite, one that Dad helped me find during our first trip to the ocean, when he taught me to swim. I remember his words the last time I saw him: "There's a lot I need to explain to you." Maybe once he does, everything will make sense and all my hurt will go away. Maybe God is finally letting something good happen.

The Spiritual Zone

After my parents separated, I had difficulty feeling close to God. I still attended church each week and prayed each night. However, God felt as far away from me as the many miles that separated me and my dad. I kept thinking, *How could God, who is supposed to love me, let my parents separate and give me all this hurt?* I was even more confused because I couldn't think of anything I had done that was so wrong that God would be punishing me like this. The only answer I could come up with was that God was ignoring me because there were more important people to look after.

We each connect with God in our own way, and I call this space of connection the "Spiritual Zone." It is a unique space for all of us, one that changes and grows as we do. What is your Spiritual Zone like? What are some of the thoughts you have when you're in the Spiritual Zone? Maybe it's tough for you to trust that God is even there. So, after a few minutes, you bolt out of the Spiritual Zone. Or maybe your Spiritual Zone is so cluttered with questions that you don't want to even enter it, or when you do, you don't know which direction to turn. Or perhaps your Spiritual Zone is such a natural place for you that you go there often.

1. QUESTIONS ARE GOOD

What questions about God does your family situation cause for you? Imagine, for a moment, that God is a friend with whom you've just had a disagreement. You call another friend to explain what's happened. What would you say about the way you feel God treated you? Write your thoughts below.

Free to Make Mistakes

It's understandable to question God's goodness and love when something bad happens. After all, when we think of someone who loves us, we think of a person who protects and cares for us, someone who wants us to be happy—not someone who lets bad things happen to us.

Yet God's love is a different kind of love than human love. It is true and perfect and not limited in the ways that human love is. An essential quality of God's love is that it frees us to be who and what we are. We are free to love—and free to mess up. Out of love, God gives us freedom, and because we're free we can make our own choices—good or bad. Our freedom also means that we live in an imperfect world. People can be awesomely good, but they can also be incredibly destructive.

The important thing to hang on to is that God wants the best for us; God does not cause or want bad things to happen, but God does promise to be with us when they do.

God did not prevent my dad from calling and seeing me more often. Nor did God make my mom so angry that she yelled at me every time I talked about missing him. Instead, my parents were the ones who were responsible for these choices. God let them do what they wanted because God gives free will. The bottom line is that God wants and wills good but allows us the freedom to make mistakes.

2. "WE ALL MAKE MISTAKES."

How well do you think your parents are using their free will to make choices? What are some good choices they've made? What are some choices that seem pretty lousy to you?

MY PARENTS' GOOD CHOICES: **MY PARENTS' LOUSY CHOICES:**

_____   _____

_____   _____

_____   _____

_____   _____

_____   _____

"Who Are You, God?"

After my parents separated, I kept God at a distance. I was too afraid to lean on God because I had believed in my parents so much—and they let me down. That made me fear that God might let me down as well. I had been taught that God made everything and loved each of us, and mostly I believed it. But I didn't understand what it meant to be connected to God—especially when I was hurting so much.

To me, God was more like Santa Claus, someone who rewards people for good behavior and punishes them for being bad. I thought God would reward me somehow for being a "good girl," but that wasn't happening. So I began to make secret bargains that went something like this: *Maybe if I go to church more often or stop fighting with my brother, God will let something go my way.*

Perhaps you make deals with God, too, or maybe you interact with God on a more personal level, as with a best friend. On the other hand, God might be someone you think of in a more abstract way, such as a force of nature or treasure to look for on your journey of life.

3. YOUR IMAGE OF GOD

There are many different ways in which people relate to God. Check (✓) any that fit you. Then put a star (*) by the image that's strongest for you.

_____ Santa Claus who rewards you for being good

_____ Superman who rescues you from trouble

_____ Mother

_____ Father

_____ Best friend

_____ Someone who loves you the most

_____ Fire that purifies you like gold

_____ Good Shepherd

_____ Judge who keeps a list of your mistakes

_____ Prosecutor

_____ Advisor

_____ Master chess-player

_____ Master craftsman

_____ Long winding path with rainbows and weeds

_____ Force or energy

_____ Other: _____

"Where Are You, God?"

It took me a long time to learn that God could not be bargained with. All of my good behavior at home and school never earned me what I wanted most: my dad to move back and my mom's hurt to be taken away. Instead, I got to know a very different God, a God who kept offering to enter into my struggles with me, a God who offered love and support. It took me a long time to get to know God like this, though, because I was stubborn and scared. My stubbornness and fear kept getting in the way, like weeds working their way into a beautiful garden. I was also more comfortable relying on myself, because it was what I usually did. That way, no one could disappoint me or screw things up.

Maybe you feel distant from God because you're afraid to give God a chance. You might be blaming God for all that's going wrong in your life. Or you might be really thankful for God right now because you believe God has helped you get through the worst.

4. "WHERE IS GOD?"

Do you think your parents' separation or divorce is moving you closer or farther away from God? Draw a stick figure or symbol on the scale below to indicate where you stand in relation to God these days.

DISTANT FROM GOD	1	2	3	4	5	6	7	8	9	10	CLOSE TO GOD

Describe some ways in which you feel distant or close:

_____

_____

_____

_____

_____

_____

Taking a Chance on God

One of the things that kept me distant from God was focusing on what I wanted *God* to do, not what God wanted *me* to do. Focusing on what I wanted didn't get me anywhere. In fact, it got me only more upset and discouraged, and I began to feel totally stuck. Then I experienced a crisis: the breakup of my first serious relationship. It was the lowest point of my life. I remember sitting alone on the floor and listening to music, feeling wiped out.

After a while, something seemed to be calling my attention. It was as though someone was tapping me gently on the shoulder and whispering, "Give me a chance." I thought that someone might be God. After a few minutes of thinking about God being there, I decided to take a chance on believing that God could help me. It made all the difference.

God did not take away my problems. However, God did give me the strength to accept the losses in my life. And I learned an important lesson: In order to give God a real chance, I had to make the first move. Here's a news alert: God won't barge into your life. Instead, God waits for you to reach out. It's a little like walking into a dark room. Is the darkness going to leave on its own? No. What we have to do is find the light switch and flip it on. It's the same way with our faith journey. We have to seek out the light, no matter how much darkness we are in.

One way in which I reach out to God is by writing a note asking for help. Then I fold up the slip of paper and tuck it in a special place. It's my way of giving my difficulties to God. Just doing that helps me feel more at peace. Then, days, weeks or months later, God sometimes surprises me. I may get an answer that wipes out my fear. A new opportunity may present itself. Or I may open one of the notes I wrote and find that the problem has been resolved without my having even realized it. God was there for me when I reached out.

5. GOD'S PLACE

Choose a place that will become your special area to leave messages for God. Then, on separate pieces of paper, write down three concerns you have right now and put them in this area. Let the place become a visual reminder that God hears you and cares about you. Let it remind you that you are not alone and that God is holding your concerns.

The Faith Factor

You've probably heard people say, "The only way out of pain is through it." But you may wonder why God seems to let you—and those you love—suffer. This problem of suffering is a mystery and goes to the heart of faith. What's most important to remember, though, is that just as suffering did not triumph over Jesus, neither will it triumph over you.

In the meantime, here are some other "faith facts" that may help you on your journey.

FAITH FACTS

FACT #1: God is not a magic eraser that eliminates problems, but God does promise to help you through them.

FACT #2: God is always working for good in your life, even when you can't see it.

FACT #3: God can work in your life only to the extent that you allow God in.

FACT #4: God's ways and timing are not the same as yours.

FACT #5: Trouble is not the time to run from God but the time to rely on God even more.

FACT #6: God has an amazing ability to transform the results of a bad situation into something good.

FACT #7: You can find meaning in suffering by asking, "What am I learning that's helping me grow and choose life?"

FACT #8: You need to see yourself as God sees you: with love.

Keep these facts in mind as you continue on your faith journey. You may want to copy and post them on your desk or keep them in your notebook. Remember, God is there and wants to help you through your difficulties. And the bottom line is that you can never become fully healed or truly whole without God.

6. EXTRA WAYS TO HELP YOURSELF

- Choose one of the "Faith Facts" and journal how it applies to your life—or how you *want* to apply it to your life.

- Think about what distances you from God. Write down some things you might do this week to help you feel closer to God, such as listening more when praying, reflecting more during church, or reaching out to a friend or family member. At the end of the week, note the things that helped most.

- In what ways do you feel that God is caring for you right now? Think especially of the people in your life who love and support you. Write a "thank you" to God for the ways God's love becomes real through other people. Read your note aloud to God.

CHAPTER TEN

Forgiveness: What If I Don't Want To?

"If you have your health, you have everything," Dad says. He narrows his brown eyes at me and adds, "That's one way our family has been very fortunate."

I force a smile, then look away. This restaurant is pretty amazing: the maitre d' pulls out the chair for you, waiters tell you the menu, and strolling violinists ask what you want to hear. All week I had been looking forward to coming here.

But Dad is ruining the evening with the way he's talking to me. I know he's trying to tell me something important, but I have no clue what it is. All I can think about is that I see him only once or twice a year now that he's divorced Mom and moved away, and here he is playing another guessing game!

"You know, Lynn, I moved away because I had to. Things with your mother and me were just getting worse. I knew there was no hope of working them out."

I nod, listening to Dad rehash the past. Details about fighting and cheating that I've already heard. Details I don't want to be reminded of. Details that have nothing to do with my life. *Doesn't Dad get any of this?*

He stares at his glass. "Moving away seemed like the best option at the time." Then he looks right at me and adds, "For everyone."

I feel like shouting, *So what's your point? Am I supposed to tell you that you did the right thing? What about all the times you didn't call? Don't you know how much that hurt?*

I glance at him. He looks up from the table and, for the first time in my life, I see tears in his eyes. "I'm sorry, Lynn. I've tried in my own way, but it just wasn't good enough. I'm sorry for all the hurt I've caused you."

I can't believe Dad is actually crying right here in the restaurant in front of me. I never knew he felt sorry about anything.

"It's okay, Dad." It's all I can think to say.

Forgiveness Is Tough

Your parents' separation or divorce may be making your life so difficult that it seems unfair that, on top of everything else, you are expected to forgive them—especially if they do not seem sorry. I had problems forgiving my parents because I was so angry and critical. I kept thinking, *I'm the one who's been wronged the most. Plus, they are older and should know better. It's up to them, not me, to patch up our relationship.*

Maybe you're having trouble forgiving because a parent keeps hurting you over and over again. Or maybe a parent has done something so terrible that you don't think he or she deserves to be forgiven. Forgiveness can even seem pointless if your parent doesn't seem to care about having a relationship with you.

1. YOUR FORGIVENESS ID

How difficult is it for you to forgive your parents for their separation/ divorce or for how they are treating you? Check (✓) all the statements below that apply to you. Then put a star (*) by your number one reason.

Forgiving my parents is tough for me because...

_____ I'll probably just get hurt again.

_____ I don't think my mom/dad deserve to be forgiven for what they've done.

_____ My mom/dad are clueless about how I feel. They act as if this is "no big deal."

_____ I don't want to face how weak and imperfect my mom/dad really are. I need them to be people I can look up to and be proud of.

_____ My mom/dad keep hurting me over and over. Why forgive them when they're just going to do it again?

_____ I don't really care. It's their problem. I don't need to forgive any-body.

_____ Other: _____

A Closer Look

Now, let's take a closer look at what's making it difficult for you to forgive. Read the paragraphs that match the statements you checked.

- **I'll probably just get hurt again.**

  Sometimes a parent will continue to hurt us, no matter what we do. When this happened with my parents, it was because their weak-nesses got in the way. This didn't mean I didn't have to forgive them, though. Instead, it meant I had to protect myself in the process by setting boundaries. If this fits for you, review the section on "Off Limits!" on page 84 in Chapter 5.

- **I don't think my mom/dad deserve to be forgiven for what they've done.**

  Early in life we are taught that wrongs should be punished. When parents separate or divorce, though, it can seem as if one (or both) of them has gotten away with something. This is especially true if your parent has not apologized.

  Unfortunately, some parents never say they are sorry. They might not even try to do better in the future, either. However, we don't need to be their judge—God will see to it that justice is done. It may be helpful for you to find an adult whom you trust to help you sort out your conflicting feelings about your parents: your anger for what they've done and your need to still love—and be loved by—them.

- **My mom/dad are clueless about how I feel. They act as if this is "no big deal."**

  Remember, your parents are likely hurt and angry and experiencing other negative feelings, just as you are. Being in "emotional overload" may cause them to tune out your feelings because they have reached their limit. Try to be patient with them and, when the time is right, let them know in a helpful way how you feel. If you find yourself in this situation, review exercise **"4. What's Your Plan?"** in Chapter 5.

- **I don't want to face how weak and imperfect my mom and dad really are. I need them to be people I can look up to and be proud of.**

  All of us have weaknesses and imperfections because we are human. Part of growing up means seeing our parents as real people with both strengths and weaknesses. Learn as much as you can about your parents' upbringing and who they are. It will help you understand and empathize with them, which will make it easier to move toward forgiveness.

- **My mom/dad keep hurting me over and over. Why forgive them when they're just going to do it again?**

  This is a very valid reason. If your parents keep hurting you, you need to set a boundary or limit to protect yourself from getting hurt repeatedly. Go back and check out the "Off Limits!" section on page 84 in Chapter 5 again to help you set some boundaries that will protect you.

- **I don't really care. It's their problem. I don't need to forgive anybody.**

  If you feel this way, you have been hurt very much. However, when you cling to anger, instead of working through it, it weakens you like a disease. Forgiveness is the best medicine for anger. Consider getting some help from an adult you trust—a teacher, a pastor, a counselor. You might want to spend extra time on Chapter 8, "Anger," too.

Fact or Fiction?

When I was growing up, I did not understand what forgiveness really meant. This lack of understanding was a big factor that held me back from forgiving my parents. What is your forgiveness IQ? Take this quiz and find out.

2. YOUR FORGIVENESS IQ

Circle "True" or "False" for each statement.

a) Forgiving someone means you must no longer be angry or have other negative feelings toward him or her.	True	False
b) If you forgive, you have to become close to the person who hurt you.	True	False
c) You do not have to forgive an immoral person.	True	False
d) You may want to forgive someone but not be ready to.	True	False
e) Forgiving is a necessary part of healing.	True	False
f) You cannot forgive until the offender asks for it or shows that he or she is sorry.	True	False
g) When you forgive others, you show that you believe that God has forgiven you.	True	False
h) If you forgive someone, you have to forget what they've done.	True	False

Check out your perceptions against the answers below. Broadening your understanding of what forgiveness is—and isn't—can go a long way toward helping you mend your relationship with your parent(s).

a) **Forgiving someone means you must no longer be angry or have other negative feelings toward him or her.**

FALSE. Even once you forgive, you will probably have to work a while on settling your negative feelings, such as anger or resentment. The feelings often stay around long after the wrong act itself. Forgiveness does not mean you have to bury negative feelings, but rather recognize them for what they are.

b) **If you forgive, you have to become close to the person who hurt you.**

FALSE. You may want to become close to the person who hurt you (this is called reconciliation), especially when that person is your parent. However, this is not always possible.

c) **You do not have to forgive an immoral person.**

FALSE. It is difficult enough to forgive, let alone forgive someone who trashes good and seems to revel in the bad. However, God wants us to forgive all persons.

d) **You may want to forgive someone but not be ready to.**

TRUE. Forgiveness can take a long time to achieve. It may be an effort you need to make over and over again.

e) **Forgiving is a necessary part of healing.**

TRUE. Forgiveness allows you to find peace, both with your parents and yourself.

f) **You cannot forgive until the offender asks for it or shows that he or she is sorry.**

FALSE. Forgiving someone who does not say or show that he or she is sorry is very hard. However, when you choose to forgive such a person, you are choosing not to let negative feelings consume you, so you can move on with your life.

g) **When you forgive others, you show that you believe that God has forgiven you.**

TRUE. Forgiving others is a sign of God's ongoing action in the world.

h) **If you forgive someone, you have to forget what they've done.**

FALSE. Forgiving doesn't mean forgetting or excusing what has happened. God wants us to have realistic expectations of others and to set boundaries with difficult people. To do this, we need to remember and learn from the past. This helps to prevent us from getting hurt by the same situation over and over again.

The Cost of Not Buying In

Now, let's regroup and look at forgiveness from another angle, maybe one you've never really considered before: What might happen if you don't forgive your parents?

In the opening story, forgiving my father was the furthest thing from my mind. Instead, I clung to anger over all my dad was not doing for me. This kept me distanced from him. It also got me angrier and prevented me from getting to know who he really was.

Maybe you've already noticed this domino effect of not forgiving. Perhaps one of your parents has picked up on this and has stopped calling or seeing you as often. This, in turn, may have caused you more hurt and anger and pushed you further away from him or her. By refusing to forgive, you may have even made yourself so bummed out that your friends have stopped hanging out with you as much.

3. RISK FACTORS

What are some of the negative results that might happen if you don't forgive your parent(s)? Note any that may have happened already, as well as any you can imagine happening in the future.

_____

_____

_____

_____

_____

_____

Taking the High Road

What helped me the most in forgiving my parents was trying to stand in their shoes. My dad helped me do this when he told me about himself and cried in front of me. I began to understand things about him that I had never realized before. I saw that he was a man with weaknesses—some of them big ones. This showed me that he could not give me what I had been hoping for. Instead of getting angry at him for it, though, I realized that it was out of his control.

It was the same with my mom. At times, she told me about her upbringing and, gradually, I tried to imagine the decisions I would have made if I were in her shoes. I began to see the difficulties she faced as a teenager and later as a young adult—ones that were very different from the ones I had experienced. It made me realize that in many ways my mom had a much tougher road than I did.

This awareness did not take away the hurt, but it lessened it. I felt more at peace, too, because I understood my parents' situations better. My anger began to turn into compassion.

A good way to stand in each of your parent's shoes and forgive him or her more fully is to write a forgiveness letter—even if you never send it.

4. THE FORGIVENESS LETTER
You will need 6 pieces of paper total, 3 for each parent.

Consider, first, the parent with whom you're having the most trouble.

1) Start your letter with your real feelings: "I am angry because…" or "I am hurt because.…" Be as specific as you can about how your parent has hurt you in the past. Remember to stay focused on your side of things.

NOTE: If your parent is continuing to hurt you in the present, you need to set a boundary first. If you are in this situation, review the exercise **"4. What's Your Plan?"** in Chapter 5. You can then return to the Forgiveness Letter in the future, after you have established solid boundaries with your parent.

2) Now take out a separate piece of paper and move to another place to write. Jot down this statement: "I understand that…." Write about the weaknesses or problems that you think may have caused your parent to do what he or she did. If you're not sure or need help, write some questions to help you understand your parent's side.

3) Using another piece of paper, complete your letter with this sentence: "I forgive you for…." Include anything else you want to add.

Complete steps 1, 2 and 3 for your other parent.

Please Help

Ultimately, I found that I needed God's help in order to forgive my parents. Even when I understood more about them, sometimes part of me still didn't want to forgive. Maybe you feel the same way. If so, it's okay to ask God for help. You can tell God, "I would like to forgive but I can't. Please help me."

5. "SEND MAIL"

Think of communicating with God as if you were sending an e-mail to a friend. What do you need to tell your friend? What do you want from your friend? Ask God directly for the help you need in forgiving your parents.

From:

To: God@everywhere.com

Subject:

One of Jesus' teachings is that we need to forgive others "seventy times seven times," which means to forgive *always*. Even when people were crucifying him, he cried out to God, "Forgive them. They do not know what they are doing."

In this extraordinary example, Jesus shows how you can move past your hurts by having an open heart. There are two things that can help you keep an open heart:

- Recognize that God made us all human and imperfect. When you can see people in this way, it becomes easier to forgive them. You can remember that others were not at their best when they hurt you and that they are more than their failings.

- Realize that God will never abandon you and is always ready to forgive you. When you allow that forgiveness in, God's grace will help you forgive others.

Forgiving may be one of the toughest jobs that you ever have to do. Opening your heart may mean possibly getting hurt again. But opening your heart is also what makes room for the good stuff—like inner peace and happiness and love. Forgiveness is the ultimate connection—with parents who have hurt you, with yourself, and with God. It's yours for the giving.

6. EXTRA WAYS TO HELP YOURSELF

- Do something that shows one of your parents that you have forgiven him/her. Consider things such as giving your parent your forgiveness letter, telling him/her about your forgiveness, or simply saying you're sorry for his/her pain. Then notice any positive changes that may result in your relationship.

- Read the story of the crucifixion and death of Jesus in the Bible (see Luke 23:33-49). Then think about how Jesus may be calling you to be more forgiving in your life.

- Think of a time when you experienced another's forgiveness. How did you feel? Then consider offering that gift to someone you need to forgive, starting with your parents.

A Note to Parents and Youth Leaders

This is a book for teens who have separated or divorced parents, but it's also a book for parents and youth leaders who want to help them heal and grow. You can use this material with support groups, retreats, health or religious education classes, counseling sessions, as well as with individual adolescents. If you want more information on how to establish or expand a support group or retreat program in your area, please contact me at the Faith Journeys Foundation, Inc. at P.O. Box 1222, Ellicott City, MD 21041; (410) 744-4910; www.faithjourneys.org.

As you've probably already discovered, separation and divorce hurts young people no matter how well their parents get along or how affluent their circumstances are. This book will help you guide them through their grief and other difficulties that result, whether the breakup is recent or years old.

In working with teens, it's critical to remember that they require years, if not decades, to work through the grief and problems resulting from their parents' separation or divorce. This is because their healing is intertwined with their ongoing personal development and maturation.

I was eleven years old when my parents separated, and I can confirm this lengthy healing process firsthand. Parental separation and divorce pose many challenges for teens precisely because of the unique nature of their grief. Unlike adults, the losses for teens are rarely clear-cut and defined. They are characterized, instead, by an absence of finality

One of the main goals of this book has been to help teens confront and define their losses. I have seen, through the work of my foundation, how much the sharing of personal journeys helps teens explore and honor their own journeys. So I have offered parts of my story throughout this book, and I encourage you to share your grief experiences as well.

Parental breakup will undoubtedly challenge teenagers' faith. You may hear questions such as, "Why is this happening to me? I haven't done anything wrong." Or "If God is so good and loving, why would he let me suffer like this?" I have addressed these and similar questions to help teens explore their relationship with God and to draw on God's help to handle their grief. It is important to have patience and give teens permission to express any angry or distrustful feelings they may have toward God. It's precisely this struggle that may, indeed, solidify their faith. Take advantage of the opportunity their struggle gives you to share your own faith journey with them as well.

Acknowledgments

Working with teens is challenging. Remember, though, that the rewards are equally as great. Just as Jesus embraced the cross and rose to new life, so too can we help young people do the same, leading them to experience more peace and joy than they ever imagined possible for themselves. This book became possible because of the support and effort of many people. I am profoundly grateful to all of them:

Special appreciation to my husband, George Kapusinski, who shows me each day what it means to live the faith. With his love, kindness and unwavering support, I have been able to follow my dreams and experience tremendous joy in touching the lives of young people who have separated and divorced parents. Words could never express the beauty he has given me.

To my parents and brothers, who have let me into their hearts, souls and minds over the years as they have journeyed toward wholeness. They have been my greatest teachers, and they have inspired me for a lifetime. My deep appreciation to them for all the ways they have been there for me.

To Greg Pierce, President and Co-Publisher of ACTA Publications, for his leadership and receptiveness to the idea for this book. Also to Editor Marcia Broucek who welcomed this project with an enthusiasm and dedication that heartened me. Her high editorial standards, talent and many years of experience enabled this book to be the best it could be.

To the Dioceses of Harrisburg and Pittsburgh who have invited me to lead retreats for young people over the years and to speak to parents, teachers, mentor couples and religious leaders. Also to various parishes throughout the Archdiocese of Baltimore who have given me the opportunity to lead young people's support groups. Those experiences were invaluable in shaping the content of this book.

Finally, to the countless teenagers who have entrusted their experiences to me and shared their sufferings in the hope of finding healing. They taught me in so many ways and enabled this book to be more accessible to its audience. I cannot thank them enough for the very special purpose they have given my life.